ANGELIC ATTENDANTS

WHAT REALLY HAPPENS
AS WE TRANSITION
FROM THIS LIFE INTO THE NEXT

ANGELIC
ATTENDANTS

JULIE RYAN

CLEMENT
Clement, Inc.

Clement, Inc.
2539 John Hawkins Parkway, Suite 101
Birmingham, AL 35244
www.clementinc.net

Library of Congress Control Number: 2017909599

ISBN 978-0-9991259-4-6 (pbk)
ISBN 978-0-9991259-6-0 (ebook)

10 9 8 7 6 5 4 3 2 1

First Edition: June 2017

Printed in the United States of America

This book is dedicated
to my mother Mary Jo Ryan
who through her dying process
gave me the opportunity to witness
firsthand the glorious adventure
we will all experience.

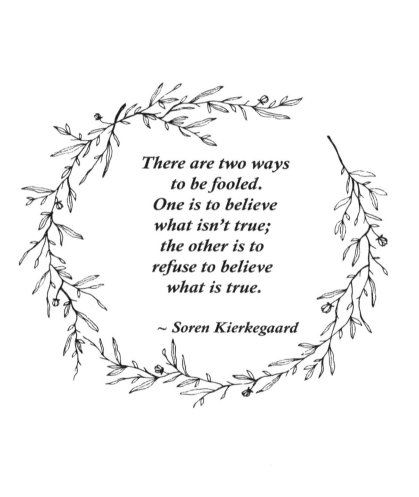

*There are two ways
to be fooled.
One is to believe
what isn't true;
the other is to
refuse to believe
what is true.*

~ Soren Kierkegaard

Contents

Preface

*W*hat *really* happens when we die? Do our deceased loved ones come for us? Do we feel an urge to move toward the light? Are there angels and trumpets and the swinging open of heavenly gates? Many people wonder about and even debate these scenarios—but not me. I *know*. I know because I've seen it myself, time and time again.

I'm psychic. Basically, I can sense what medical conditions and illnesses a person has, I can facilitate energetic healings, I can see energy fields—and I can communicate with spirits both alive and dead. One of the most rewarding parts of what I do is witnessing people making their transitions on their deathbeds. Losing a loved one is always painful, but when I describe what's happening on the spirit level—including the arrival of angels and deceased family members' spirits who come to greet and support the dying person (often including details I could not possibly have known any other way)—the family feels enormously comforted. It's always an honor and a privilege.

The fear of not knowing what will happen at death to a loved one (or to ourselves, for that matter) is natural. The list of questions seems endless:

- What happens to our bodies? Do we have a soul?

- Are we spirits in bodies or bodies attached to spirits?
- Is there a sequence of events that transpires in the process of dying?
- Is dying scary?
- What is the "tunnel" seen by people who have had near-death experiences?
- Do we have any control over when and how we go?
- Do we see our deceased loved ones as we die?
- Do angels really exist and do they assist us at death?
- Does Heaven exist, and how do we get there?
- Do our pets join us in the afterlife?
- Can loved ones who have passed on see us and hear us if we try to talk to them?

In fact, the desire for a spiritual explanation of death has never been greater, especially for baby boomers—the inquisitive generation. We boomers like to have control of our lives and our environment, and we often find not knowing an outcome to be frightening. We're logical thinkers who are fascinated by the possibility of the spirit world. While some of us continue to attend the traditional organized-religion churches we knew as children, we now find a way to integrate religion and spirituality. For many of us, the days of blindly doing what the clergy tells us to do are over.

Religious beliefs about death and dying (not to mention about most of life's experiences) have been passed down through the ages, in some instances for millennia.

These beliefs were originally formulated for a variety of reasons, some altruistic and some controlling. Often when we turn to religion for answers, we're left feeling perplexed when we're told, "Death is a mystery."

I was raised Roman Catholic, and I've always felt comforted by the prayer called *In Paradisum* (Latin for "into paradise") said at the end of every Catholic funeral. This prayer, believed to have originated in the fifth century as a Gregorian chant, best describes what I psychically see when witnessing the dying process. The translation of this prayer is:

In peace let us take our brother/sister to their place of rest.

May the angels lead you into paradise; may the martyrs come to welcome you and take you to the Holy City, the new and eternal Jerusalem.

May choirs of angels welcome you and lead you to the bosom of Abraham; and where Lazarus is poor no longer, may you find rest.

Over the past many years I've often wondered if the artists and writers of long ago could "see" what I see when someone dies. Think of all the old masters' paintings where a person has a halo over their head or a ring of light around their body. Is this their spirit? Today, we may hear people refer to this as a person's energy field. And what about all those angels around people in paintings that appear to be dying, either in battle, at home, or elsewhere?

Was it more common for people of ancient civilizations

to be able to tune into their psychic abilities? What about the Australian Aborigines—they have communicated telepathically over great distances for thousands of years. Have we, with the need for instantaneous validation/proof and access to massive amounts of online information become so skeptical that we've shut down a natural ability that most of our ancestors possessed?

Just because we can't see, feel, hear, or smell something doesn't mean it isn't real. After all, how often do we question whether or not our modern conveniences really work? Have you ever seen the energy a microwave oven uses to cook food? How about the energy a smartphone uses to allow us to talk to, text, and email one another?

Scientists have been conducting experiments on energy for quite some time, and those studies are getting increasingly more detailed and meaningful. For example, we now have the technology to detect and quantify what's happening when one person sends energy to another. Likewise, medical research has been able to pinpoint what region of the brain (the frontal lobe) is involved when a person like me experiences what's known as "non-local reality," or being in more than one place at a time and actually seeing (psychically) what is transpiring in the other place.

Will we ever be able to scientifically explain what I see happening in the spiritual plane when people die and make their transitions to another reality? Maybe, or maybe not. Either way, witnessing this intricately orchestrated process, combined with the immense respect I feel for the person who is dying, fills me with awe and wonder every time. It never gets old. Nor does the deep appreciation families seem to have when I share what I experience with them.

The information I'm able to convey can bring peace at a time that seems filled with anything but peace, and those who stay open inevitably end up discovering a new way to embrace life through what they learn about the experience of death.

Prodding From A Dead Pope

After I first started to understand the death and dying process, the question of how best to share this information was always floating around in the back of my mind. One day, while I was with my mentor, teacher and dear friend Susan Austin Crumpton, the spirit of a deceased pope appeared in front of us in full papal attire. I asked him who he was, and he replied, "Clement."

"There was a Pope Clement?" I responded in surprise.

"I was number 6," he told me with a chuckle.

Pope Clement VI went on to tell me I just needed to do what I was born to do—educate people around the world about what happens as a person is dying and how there isn't anything to fear. Clement went on to say that everything I'd previously done in business was training for what lay ahead.

When I researched Pope Clement VI, I found he had been in office during the era of the Bubonic Plague that killed an estimated 60 percent of Europe's population in the 14th century. Not surprisingly, Clement is best known for his care of and prayers for the dying and dead. Since his first visit, Pope Clement has become one of my spirit guides, continuously advising, prodding, and encouraging me to engage in what he continued to call my life's mission. Although I initially resisted, after years of seeing how this information could completely transform someone's experience of watching a loved one die, I found the courage to accept the task and began the journey of educating the world about what happens as we transition from this life into the next.

Part I

Background

Chapter 1

My Story

I didn't always see dead people and angels. In fact, my early life was fairly normal. Born in the late 1950s to upper-middle-class, college-educated parents, I grew up in Columbus, Ohio, during the middle of the Baby Boom. The second of four children, I was raised in a traditional home and received 12 years of private Catholic school education before earning a bachelor's degree from The Ohio State University.

I've always been naturally curious about everything. I'm interested in travel, art, human nature, music, architecture, business, different cultures, landscaping, medical discoveries, history, astronomy—you name it, and I want to learn about it. My constant curiosity causes my husband to affectionately call me an "information suck"!

School however, wasn't ever enjoyable. For the most part, I found it extremely tedious—unless of course, I happened to be interested in the subject being discussed. Sitting in a class-room all day hearing someone lecture about something, read-ing the same material when I got home that night, trying to memorize it, and then spewing it back on a test convinced me that there *must* be a better way. Even though my grades were mostly C's with a few A's and B's thrown in, I would score very high on standardized tests, especially in the language arts categories. My parents would tell me I was just lazy and didn't apply myself. Perhaps. What they failed to realize was that I was just bored out of my mind. I knew intellectually I had to go to school, get decent grades and eventually graduate, but I found having to go through the process exhausting.

For some reason, my senior year in high school was my best year academically. I managed to design a schedule of classes in history, literature, and other subjects that interested me. That one year, I received all A's and made the National Honor Society. My parents were thrilled—and astounded. I didn't much care, except I knew my academic accomplishments would help me get into a sorority during the upcoming fall rush at Ohio State.

Some bored kids become behavior problems. Not I, unless you count the time I was sent to the principal's office in the seventh grade for shooting rubber bands. Unfortunately, mine hit my teacher in the butt, and although the class thought it was hilarious, he didn't and sent me to the principal's office. The funniest part of that story, however, was the principal happened to be my mother. After learning of my crime, she had a tough time maintaining a straight face. She kept saying, "My own flesh and blood has been sent to the office for misbehaving." I'm not sure I even received a punishment. She probably told me to be good and to put the roast in the oven when I got home from school.

Even though I didn't like the structure and format of traditional school, I did enjoy its social aspects. Lunch, recess, and gym were the bright spots of my day because they allowed me to talk with my friends. Those parts of school, plus writing notes in class about whatever drama was currently unfolding (and passing those notes along secretive pathways, under desks and hidden beneath people's hands, while managing to not get caught) and spending hours on the phone at night rehashing the world-shattering event of the day (like who said what to whom, and which boy was going with one of my friends) was my saving grace.

Doing It My Way

I wasn't necessarily always compliant. If something didn't make sense to me, I'd argue my point with the infallible wisdom of a child. I'd usually lose, but it made me feel better for at least trying. In retrospect, I now see I was developing what some call critical thinking along with problem solving techniques that would serve me for the rest of my life. Even now, I do my best to look at all sides of a situation. The bird's eye view helps me to have understanding and compassion for the other person. It also helps me consider a different viewpoint that when combined with my opinion can make a situation better.

Consequently, in my adult life, I've always done things a little differently from the masses. When I was told something I envisioned couldn't be done, I'd usually find a way to make it happen. When obstacles were put in my path, I told myself it was just an opportunity to make a change that would result in a better outcome, and then I'd do my best to find a way. When everyone went right, I often times went left. I figured the path less traveled had benefits. There'd be less competition, less rigid principles for how to do something, and more opportunity to forge something new.

Right out of college I went to work as a rep selling hospital supplies for a publicly traded, multi-billion-dollar company. By the age of 25, I had started my first company and within a couple of years had invented an orthopedic surgery device. My product collected a patient's blood after they'd received a new knee or hip joint and then gave the patient's own blood back to them after surgery. The technology was licensed to the largest global orthopedic device company on the planet, and after 25 years, it's still being sold throughout the world.

I've had companies in the long-term care, nursing home, and natural gas industries. I've been in the advertising field and medical device manufacturing business. And for the past several years, the corporate data breach prevention arena has captured my attention and spawned a couple of businesses. In the past 30 years, I've started nine successful companies from scratch, and I've been granted several patents and trademarks on products I've invented. Although that sounds like it was easy for me, my entrepreneurial life had its share of ups and downs. I've lived through times when I didn't know where my next $100 was coming from and times with a monthly six-figure income. I've fought legal battles with business partners violating agreements and had to deal with the FDA auditing my medical device company.

Through it all, I saw each venture as an adventure. To me, structure is about 10 percent of any equation. Creativity and ingenuity are the other 90 percent. It didn't matter what industry I was working in, what mattered to me was going wherever I was led.

So you see, I'm an inventor and a serial entrepreneur. I'm not a typical woo-woo psychic who's had dead people stalking her since childhood. I'm a businesswoman who happens to also have psychic abilities, and I've had some success at both through a combination of God-given talents along with allowing myself to access information in non-traditional ways.

Unknown Abilities

Although I didn't always know I had psychic abilities, looking back on my life I do recall times when I was indeed aware of knowing something without being able to explain how I knew it. One example happened on April 19, 1995. As I was getting dressed that morning at my Los Angeles home, I turned on the television and saw initial reports from Oklahoma City where a bomb had just exploded. The panic I watched on TV matched the panic I felt inside my body—not just because of the horror of the scene, but also because I knew one of my dearest friends had been hurt in the explosion. Patty McCarthy Labarthe and I have been friends since we were 10 years old. Even though I didn't know the exact location of the destroyed buildings, I knew Patty's office was somewhere in downtown

Oklahoma City, and after repeated unanswered calls to her office, cell phone, and home, I knew she was in trouble.

I ran downstairs and found my husband. By this time, I was crying so hard I could barely speak and my heart was beating so fast that it felt as though it would leap out of my chest. After I blurted out the story of the bombing and knowing Patty had been injured, my husband did his best to calm me down. He asked how I knew for sure she was hurt.

"Did you talk to her?" he asked logically.

"No," I responded.

"Well then, how do you know she's injured?"

"I just *know*," I yelled back at him.

"You're nuts," he responded as lovingly as he could. "Calm down and keep trying to call her."

My fears were confirmed later that afternoon when Patty and I finally spoke via phone. She told me her office building was directly across the street from the Murrah Federal Building, where the explosion occurred.

As the bomb detonated, the powerful blast blew across the street and caused massive amounts of damage in her building. Patty described how she was sitting at her desk with her back to the window when the explosion went off. The blast shattered her window, causing shards of glass to fly inward, and forced her head down on her desk and the ceiling to collapse on top of her. The lacerations on the back of her head needed dozens of stitches, but she was alive. Thank God! After hanging up the phone, I again burst into tears. This time, however, my tears were those of relief.

I now believe my psychic abilities were the reason I knew beyond any logical thought pattern that Patty was injured. At the time, I didn't know I had any psychic abilities, let alone what I would've done with them had I been aware.

An Unlikely Reiki Master

My journey as a psychic began about 1986 when my friend Marianne Glorian Urbanos introduced me to Reiki, a form of energy healing. She was a first-generation American of Armenian descent who didn't speak English until she went to first grade. About 25 years older than me, Marianne was one of the first people I met when I moved to Los Angeles. She took me under her wing and became one of my best friends. She used to say, "I'm a piece of pumpernickel and Julie is a piece of white bread!" The woman was the epitome of a free spirit.

One day, Marianne said, "I'm a Reiki master, and I want to make you a Reiki healer." Although I'd never heard of Reiki, I trusted her and agreed to be initiated. The next thing I knew, we were in the middle of a ceremony. She lit candles, waved her arms around, and showed me pictures of Sanskrit symbols.

This is right up her alley, I thought. *I'm in the middle of some Armenian gypsy voodoo ritual.* Although I wasn't sure what I was getting myself into, I decided to go along with the initiation because it obviously meant a lot to her.

And with that, Marianne made me a Reiki healer. No instruction, no nothing—all I had to do was go through this ceremony. Afterwards, I didn't feel any differently and I didn't give Reiki much thought until a couple of years later when my mother mentioned how a nurse who had cared for her after surgery used Reiki to help ease her pain. I found it interesting that a healthcare professional was using energy healing to compliment traditional pain medication and that the practice was being done in a large metropolitan hospital. I also found it fascinating that my ultra-conservative mother welcomed and acknowledged the pain relief that came from the nurse's Reiki healing techniques.

Then one day about a year later, my 16-month-old son Jonathan and I were at a friend's house. Jonathan, who had only been walking for a short time, fell on the patio and skinned his knees. The injury wasn't severe—just a few droplets of blood on both knees along with swelling and what I assumed was the beginning of some bruising.

As I held Jonathan on my lap to comfort him, I remembered my Reiki initiation and cupped my hands over his knees. This lasted a few minutes until he wanted down to go play some more. About an hour later, as I buckled him into his car seat, I noticed there was no trace of injury to his knees—none at all! It was as if he'd never fallen. Finding this intriguing, I thought, *Well, maybe there really is something to Reiki healing.*

That incident really got my attention. I saw firsthand, with my own child, what I considered to be a spontaneous healing. After Jonathan fell, his knees were injured and tender, yet within an hour, he showed no bruising, no sign of blood, and no skinned knees. The injury was completely gone! For the next few years, I'd occasionally put my hands on sick or injured friends and family just in case this Reiki stuff kind of worked. Occasionally, I felt my hands getting warm or even hot when I placed them on someone, and I instinctively knew some kind of mojo transfer was happening.

Meeting My Mentor

After leaving Los Angeles and moving to Nashville in 1995, I met Joyce Grizzle. We were neighbors who soon became friends, and in May of 1997, Joyce gave me a book for my birthday called *Anatomy of the Spirit*. The author, Caroline Myss, refers to herself as a medical intuitive, a term I had never heard before. In the book, Myss wrote about how every illness corresponds to a pattern of emotional and psychological stresses, beliefs, and attitudes that influence corresponding areas of the human body. She wrote about similarities between the ancient wisdom of three spiritual traditions—the Hindu chakras, the Catholic Sacraments, and the Jewish Tree of Life. Myss also described how she used energy techniques and psychic ability to help diagnose and facilitate healing.

The whole idea of energy healing fascinated me, especially in light of my experiences with both Reiki and the traditional medical industry, so after finishing Myss' book, I went to the bookstore to see what else was available on the topic. Of all the books on the shelf, I found myself drawn to *Hands of Light* by Barbara Brennan, Ph.D. Brennan, a former NASA physicist, figured out how to incorporate quantum physics and some of the theories she used for rocket science to help facilitate healing and diagnose various medical conditions. She did a great job of translating high-level quantum physics into understandable English. She also founded the Barbara Brennan School of Healing in southern Florida, a specialized college for the study of hands-on energy healing and personal transformation. There, students may choose to earn a Bachelor of Science degree or a diploma in Brennan Healing Science. To my knowledge, this is the only school in the country where one can study for a Bachelor of Science degree in medical intuitive healing.

The theories, diagrams of energy fields, and protocols for enlisting the assistance of angels and other spirits in *Hands of Light* intrigued me, and I was eager to learn more. After calling the Barbara Brennan School to find out if anyone in the Nashville area was doing this kind of work, I was able to speak with a graduate of Brennan's program who ran her own school and immediately enrolled.

Over the past 20-plus years, the founder of that school, Susan Austin Crumpton, has become my mentor, teacher, and dear friend. When I think of the people who have had the most positive influence on my life, she and my maternal grandmother are at the top of the list.

In order to be accepted into the School of Healing Arts program, I had to agree to attend monthly classes, do the homework, pay thousands of dollars in tuition, and have individual counseling sessions each month with an approved therapist for an additional fee.

Here I was, a gal who hated school and believed a federal law should be passed to outlaw homework, agreeing to all the requirements and enrolling. And I wasn't even sure why I was doing this.

Higher Education

For the next three years, I dutifully attended class, read the assigned material (most of the time), and didn't experience much of anything. But I kept going.

Between six and ten of us would show up for any given session, depending on each individual's schedule. We learned about fields of energy, how the body was comprised of vibrations and frequencies of those vibrations, and how everything was connected. We also spent a lot of time talking about different personality types, including which ones were the most prevalent in our own lives and how everyone has these traits. Through it all, my own general dislike of school kept nagging at me, making me question what I was doing there.

In the meantime, I dutifully attended my monthly individual counseling sessions with Susan and benefitted greatly from them. These sessions were in the form of traditional talk psychotherapy that always ended with Susan doing an energy healing on me. I would lie on a massage table, face up, covered with a blanket, and close my eyes. It felt warm and safe. Ever since I was a small child, I have always felt the most secure when I was in my bed under the covers. Even to this day, whenever something happens that makes me feel depressed, sad, angry, and so on, I always feel better once I climb into my bed.

At the beginning of these healing sessions, I just felt relaxed. After a few months, even though my eyes were closed, I began to see colors and images of shapes that looked like designs, vortexes, and patterns. Every once in a while I felt a jolt of energy or a light buzzing sensation course through my body, but for the most part I saw things in my mind's eye. To say the least, it was both intriguing and fantastic!

As the months progressed, our class began to play around with trying to feel energy by rubbing our hands together and then holding them just a few inches apart with our palms facing each other. Most of us could feel a bit of resistance that we learned was an energy field between our hands. Then we started practicing on each other. We'd pick a partner and take turns lying on the massage table while the other person would hold their hands above the "pretend client" and we'd both make observations.

Very early on during this phase, I began to see the same colors, images, shapes, and energy fields I'd seen when Susan worked on me, and each month, my visions seemed to intensify. Most of my classmates didn't see or feel much of anything. When it was time to share our experiences with the class, I found myself recounting elaborate visions of what had just transpired. I could sense that my stories intimidated some of the others, so I started withholding most of the details to keep my classmates from feeling uncomfortable. I saved my observations for my private sessions with Susan.

As part of our homework, we had to do healings on our family and friends. My husband and son ended up being my guinea pigs. Neither of them reported feeling or seeing much, but they both humored me. At that time, Jonathan was about 4 years old, so I'd usually zap on him after we read his bedtime story and were snuggled in his bed. Although he'd quickly fall asleep, I'd benefit from the colored energy show.

After the three-year program was over, I attended the Auric Healing graduation with the thought that *something* had transpired, although I couldn't exactly say what. At the ceremony, I felt a little like a fraud and was a bit perplexed by the whole experience. I suspected I was able to transmit energy to others, but I didn't know how or why it worked. All I knew for sure was that I wanted to learn more. I was being led to learn this stuff and didn't have a clue why.

Still More Schooling

So I enrolled in the next series of classes. The three-year Kabbalah Program was open to graduates of the Auric Healing Program that I'd just completed. All I knew about the new program was that it had to do with a type of healing originating in Jewish mysticism. I'd also heard that this knowledge was so sacred that it was only taught to married male rabbis who were over 40 years old, and it was communicated only orally. There weren't any textbooks, holy scriptures, or other documents to read. Since I was a Catholic female under 40, I didn't fit into any of the ancient required categories (except for being married). I felt like I was about to enter a magical world. I was ready for the next adventure and curious to see how it would impact, and hopefully enhance my abilities as well as see where all of it would lead.

Kabbalah comes from the Hebrew root *kabal*, which means "to receive." It's about relationship and how we communicate, one soul to another. We not only receive from one another, I learned, but we receive the creative force of God. Many experts in the field have said that meditation and other Kabbalistic concepts help us learn how to be receivers.

This class, like the auric series, was a combination of lectures, reading, and practicing on one another; it cost thousands of dollars and it required individual counseling sessions each month with an approved therapist. And again, although I didn't feel like I was learning any useful techniques, my abilities to see energy, shapes, and colors intensified. Midway through my first year of the course, I began seeing internal body parts like organs, bones, ligaments, and blood vessels. It was as if I had a big screen TV in my head and I was looking at CT-scans, x-rays, and MRIs. It was wild, and at the same time very exciting.

At first, the pictures I received from a body scan reminded me of an architectural blueprint of a home or building, with a lot of thin blue lines almost in a grid configuration. I was able to see tears in the blue lines that would correspond to ligament or muscular tears. I could see blocked arteries, shapes of tumors, and more. It wasn't as though I was doing anything special, except as I prepared to scan someone, I envisioned a wave of yellowish-white energy enter my feet, rush through my body and out the top of my head like a geyser. Then I'd close my eyes and focus on my friend, classmate, or family member. Often, I stood with my hands on their feet while they were lying on a couch or bed and then I'd watch the show in my head. It normally took less than a couple seconds for me to get the picture in my mind. At that point, all of my scans were done in person.

I continued to attend the classes, enjoy my one-on-one private sessions, and just let things unfold. It wasn't as if I was learning a technique. It was more like I was absorbing the energy frequencies Susan transmitted to me. Similar to my Reiki initiation, I wasn't given a guide showing me how to do the energy work, I mostly came up with my own techniques and nuances. And I instinctively knew the process would be a marathon not a sprint. I didn't know when or even if the process would end or how long it would take. I was beginning to understand how my imagination and creativity were serving me in the spiritual healing journey just as they had throughout my schooling and business life.

I began to recognize certain patterns. Viral infections looked like a watery brownish liquid filling the outline of a person's body. Bacterial infections were always hot pink and hovered over the infected area of the body. Cancer looked like black uneven spots (much like those seen on black and white dairy cows) on a body area. When I saw the black spots in different areas, I knew the cancer had spread or metastasized to another area of the body. Broken bones look like cracks in a bone, similar to how they appear on x-rays. Torn ligaments look like shredded pieces of crabmeat. A sprain looks like a blue ball of thin yarn. Inflammation looks like a red dry mist over the injured body part.

These and other conditions would appear in my head in order of severity. The energy always focused on the most pressing issue. Oftentimes people would tell me something hurt and the energy would go to another part of the body that needed more attention. For that reason, I'd just shoot energy into the person from the feet up through the top of their head and watch to see what came up. Then I'd tell the client what I was seeing in my head. I never edited any information I received. My belief was (and still is) who am I to judge what I need to tell or not tell the person I'm scanning? I believe I'm the conduit, the messenger, and if I'm getting the information, I'm supposed to share it.

Starting to See Spirits

In the fall of 2001, I began seeing spirits, primarily while lying on the table in Susan's office as I received a healing from her. The spirits look just like we've all seen spirits portrayed in the movies—more or less transparent holograms of a person, usually dressed in clothing from the time period in which they lived. They communicate with me telepathically, seeming to go about their business in a normal manner as though multiple realities—mine in this world and theirs in their world—exist at the same time.

I can't say I've ever been afraid of these spirits. Rather, I've always been fascinated with them. Sometimes when a new one enters the room, I'll get goose bumps, or I might see a fleeting figure out of the corner of my eye. But most of the time I don't detect them unless my radar is on. And even then, I primarily "see" spirits. Every once in a while I'll smell a scent or fragrance when a spirit is present. One day when Jonathan was in fifth grade, he told me during our drive home from school, "I smelled Nana's perfume today when I was taking my math test." I told him that maybe she wanted him to know she was there to help him. I found it interesting that the spirit of my recently deceased mother, who had been a teacher and principal, chose to let her grandson know she was close by during his test.

One of the first recognizable spirits I encountered was my paternal grandmother, Mary Alma Ryan. Grandma Ryan appeared to me as she looked in her mid-30s, dressed in 1930's attire and walking through what looked like a botanical garden. Although she didn't say anything, she looked directly at me, smiled, nodded, and then walked off down the path into another section of the garden. It was as if she just wanted to acknowledge the fact that I could see her. She looked tranquil and beautiful, just like the pictures I'd seen of her at that age. That experience seemed to open a new pathway in my ability to see and communicate with the deceased.

Within a few months, my maternal grandmother, Julia Cline (we called her Memaw or Mem for short), died and I developed another new ability. While visiting Mem in the hospital, I did a quick scan and saw an energetic bubble hooked onto the top of her head. Although I'd heard Susan talk about the spirit bubble over someone's head as they were dying, I discounted what I saw because Mem seemed to be doing better. She was coherent, even a bit talkative, and she was hungry. I fed her a roast beef dinner and dessert, and she even drank a full cup of coffee. This would be the last time I disregarded the spiritual information I received. Mem died a couple of hours later.

The following month while at Susan's I saw a scene take place in an ancient stone chapel. Mem looked to be in her late 20s, dressed as a 1920's bride in a floor-length white gown. She wore a thin white lace veil that covered the top of her head and flowed into a 10-foot train behind her. She carried a bouquet of white roses, hydrangeas, gardenias, and stephanotis. Bright sunlight streamed in through clear leaded glass windows as she walked on a white runner down the aisle of an empty chapel. I felt like I was watching a movie in which Mem was the star. It was a beautiful scene and it reminded me of the part of *The Sound of Music* when Maria walks down the aisle at her wedding. I was amazed, intrigued, and comforted by the image. Susan said Mem was going through a type of 'completion of a journey' ceremony. The vision ended before she got to the front of the chapel. I believe my Memaw was showing me she was progressing in her soul's journey. She wanted me to know she was content and at peace and that she would allow me to participate in her new reality whenever I chose to do so.

Within six months, I would be present at the death of

Mem's daughter, my mother (a story I tell in the next chapter). That, too, would open up a whole new phase in my abilities.

Fine Tuning the Lessons

During the more than 20 years that I've been involved in spiritual healing, I've realized that everyone has the ability to do this work. We don't need to learn any special techniques or use any crystals, pyramids, candles, incense, or talismans. It's about a transfer of energy from one person to another. As we become more open to the process, our abilities grow organically. As long as we stay unbiased in what we're seeing, feeling, hearing, sensing, and knowing, we have the ability to go far beyond our five senses into an unlimited field of information, understanding, and miracles. Over the years, I've found that when I focused on a particular outcome, I seemed to stop the energy flow. It's almost as if I'm closing the conduit that allows healing to occur. Staying open not to what I think is best but what Spirit's highest will for that person might be is the key. After all, what we humans think defines healing— the eradication of an illness or injury—isn't the only type of healing taking place. Sometimes, a healing isn't visible. And sometimes it doesn't happen instantaneously—it could happen days, weeks, or months later. Healing can take place even if the pain and sickness continues, even if the person dies from their illness or injury. What I do know for sure, however, is that everyone receives a healing, and that healing is exactly what they need at that particular time in their life.

Throughout many years of study and practice, I have learned how to use and continuously improve my psychic ability to scan a person's energy field in order to see (in my mind's eye) medical conditions. I've learned how to turn my abilities on and off at will, so I don't go around scanning everyone I see. I first get their permission either verbally or psychically, and when I don't get permission, I don't scan. It's an ethical issue for me. (I also don't have a desire to know about everyone.)

I have learned how to psychically see many conditions, among them broken bones, torn ligaments, viral and bacterial infections, cancer and other diseases, brain tumors—basically any type of medical condition. I have witnessed many energetic healings in the form of surgeries, organ transplants, and the repair of bone fractures and torn ligaments. I can remotely scan anyone (again, with their permission) in any location throughout the world, and I am often called upon to do so.

And, like with the Health Insurance Portability and Accountability Act (HIPAA), I keep everything I see and discuss with clients absolutely confidential.

Expanded Communication

In addition, unlike psychics who seem to talk only with dead people, I can communicate with the spirits of people who are alive. I believe what's actually happening is my spirit converses with their spirit. This can happen with anyone, not only a dying person. I can psychically ask a living person anywhere in the world a question, and I normally get an answer—one that often proves to be correct. The only thing I can equate this with is the telepathic communication used for thousands of years by the Australian Aboriginal tribes.

I also have the ability to communicate with animals, and I can scan them for medical and behavioral conditions. Among others, horses, birds, dogs, and cats have all told me about injuries, aches and pains, being hungry, or needing to go outside to do their business. I can also tell when a pet is dying and relay messages from them to their owners.

After so many years, this psychic communication has become second nature to me. Many people tell me they're fascinated by my scans, and young people seem to most easily accept what I do along with the information I receive. I wonder if it's because teenagers and young adults are less brainwashed about why something cannot be possible, leaving them more open to non-conventional thinking.

My son Jonathan, who is now an adult, is so used to the psychic side of me that it's completely normal to him, his long-time girlfriend Mallory, and most of his buddies. His close friends, now scattered across the country at different universities and jobs, will often contact me when they're feeling ill. I'll get a text message that will read something like, "Miss Julie, my throat hurts. Can you scan me and let me know if I need to go to the doctor for antibiotics?" Of course, it's my pleasure to do so. I love hearing from them, regardless of the reason.

Also, since I've been doing this for so long, many of my relatives' and friends' adult children are now parents who call requesting that I scan their children. My stepdaughter Holly often calls asking me to check out one of our grandsons. Eli, Max, and Sam are all close in age and are invariably either sick from something they caught at school or hurt from various little-boy antics. One morning, Holly called and mentioned four-year-old Sam had fallen off the swing set and was complaining about his arm hurting. I scanned him from my home a few miles away and told Holly I saw a fracture above his elbow on his right arm. I then told her I'd meet her at Children's Hospital. Sure enough, Sam had a broken arm and the x-rays showed the fracture was indeed right where I saw it.

Throughout the years, I've scanned many people for medical conditions—including family and friends as well as strangers who have asked for my help. Most people are referred to me from someone who has either worked with me or knows someone who has, and I now do 99 percent of my scans remotely.

I use my intuitive abilities every day in many areas of my life. I ask questions about business, relationships, and even the weather. When I listen to the answer that arrives within a second or two, it's normally correct. When I disregard the guidance, I always regret it.

We all have a knowing or a sense of what to do in every situation. Some people call it intuition, guidance, God, the universe, or our soul talking to us. I believe it's a combination of all of the above.

Chapter 2

My Introduction to Angelic Escorts

$\mathcal{I}$n 2002, my abilities took on a new dimension—one that gave me a unique perspective on the process of dying. I had never really thought much about what happens at the time of death. I hadn't ever been around anyone in their final stages of life. Sure, I'd been to several wakes and funerals over the years, seen families mourn, and believed the recently departed person was either in Heaven or headed there.

But just six months after losing my beloved, almost-100-year-old grandmother (we called her Memaw—or Mem for short), her daughter, my mother, Mary Jo Ryan, was admitted to a hospice facility. The call from my older brother Jay came on a Friday afternoon as I was getting my hair cut. I took the phone into the hallway of the hair salon and heard the news that my mother was dying. She had been in the hospital for a variety of reasons but I had no idea she was bad enough to call in hospice. I told my brother we'd be there as soon as possible.

That evening, my husband Tim, Jonathan (who was 10 at the time), and I drove all through the night from Birmingham,

Alabama, to Columbus, Ohio—a 10-hour drive—to get to her. Tim would drive a few hours while I slept and then I'd drive while Tim rested. We made a bed for Jonathan in the back seat.

Upon our arrival early on Saturday morning, we found my mother in a non-communicative state, lying in bed with the family around her. She moved her head when we said hello and that was the extent of her greeting. The Kobacker House hospice facility and its staff were fabulous. They told us that since my mother had arrived well hydrated from all of the intravenous fluids she'd received in the hospital, she could last a week or more. So we all settled in.

Throughout the day, as more family arrived, a somewhat surreal scene ensued. My siblings and I hadn't ever been through the dying process with anyone, let alone a loved one, so we weren't sure what to expect. Even though my dad, brothers, and sister knew I did some sort of scanning psychic woo-woo thing, it didn't occur to any of us just how useful it would become in helping us get through my mother's passing.

Now, when I look back at that time, it makes perfect sense to me that my mother (who was an elementary school teacher and then for most of her career, a principal) would give me the opportunity to learn about the dying process as she herself approached death. What a parting gift she gave both to me and to those whose lives I've touched with this material.

Several times throughout that day, my dad led us in prayer. He read from the Catholic *Prayers for the Dying*, we said the Rosary, and we also said our own individual prayers.

At one point as we were praying, I closed my eyes and psychically saw an iridescent mist floating around the room. The most interesting part was this mist was dry. It sparkled and swirled throughout my mother's entire room. When the praying stopped, the mist disappeared. It was a magical, spiritual sight. (I now believe the iridescent mist is what religious scholars call grace.) I'd never seen anything like that before. I decided to see what else I could "see" with my eyes closed. Boy, was I in for an education!

When I engaged my psychic abilities, I noticed my mother had what looked like a bright white bubble (like where the text is placed in a cartoon) attached to the top of her head. I'd heard my mentor Susan talk about how the spirit exits the body through the top of the head and how this looks like a cartoon-caption bubble, but this was the first time I'd ever actually seen and *acknowledged* one. (Remember, I saw the spirit bubble when my grandmother was dying and thought I was imagining it.)

As the day progressed, additional spiritual revelations occurred. Memaw's spirit appeared at my mother's left foot. Shortly thereafter, my mother's father appeared next to her right foot. When she was alive, Mem loved and doted on her grandkids, but in this situation, she didn't so much as glance at any of us in the room. Mem seemed to have a laser-like focus on her daughter and appeared to be directing what was happening with the spirit-world side of my mother's dying process. How touching is that? We mothers think our jobs are through once our children are raised and have become adults.

What I saw that day, and have seen many times since, is that a mother's job is never done. We even protect and assist our children from the spirit world after we're dead!

Next, many angels appeared and encircled my mother's bed. My grandparents (her parents), were still at her feet and were part of the circle. It was as if they were anchoring the angels. In addition, many spirits of deceased loved ones began to arrive and take positions behind the ring created by my grandparents and the angels. I recognized some of the spirits, mainly from family pictures, and I knew they were relatives and friends of my mother's family. Her grandparents, aunts and uncles, and various friends' spirits arrived to lend support. I watched all of this with curiosity and wonder.

While I wasn't surprised to see the spirits of my mother's family and friends, I was totally amazed to also see the spirit of our parish priest. Father Byrne had been dead for more than 25 years, and I hadn't thought of him since I'd heard he passed. He was the pastor of the church and Catholic grade school my siblings and I attended. He was also my mother's boss for the more than 20 years she was the principal at his parish's school. At first, I was surprised to see Father Byrne, but when I thought about it, his presence made sense. He had been an important part of my mother's life for many years. The other interesting point to me was that Father Byrne appeared as he did when we were children, wearing the long black cassock with Roman collar he always wore. (I now realize spirits oftentimes appear in a way we'll recognize them.)

Other spirits continued to arrive. The spirits of our white

German shepherd, Frosty, our Dachshund Schatzie and our Chow Rummy appeared along with several other dogs I didn't recognize. I later learned the other dogs were pets my mother had while growing up. (After Mother's funeral, I described the dogs I didn't recognize to my uncle Bob, Mother's brother. He named every one of them.) These animal spirits congregated in a pack to the right side of the human spirits. The dogs all sat at attention and looked as if they were guarding my mother. Although Native American lore talks about how animal spirits guide us, never in my wildest dreams did I ever imagine I'd see a bunch of dog spirits present as my mother lay dying!

In the meantime, I continued to psychically communicate with my mom. Frequently, I asked her if she was ready to go (I got a "yes" to that) and if she was in pain or if she needed anything (to which she answered "no").

The Angels Intensify

As family members continued to arrive to say goodbye, I continued to watch the happenings in the spirit world with amazement. For one, it looked as if my mother's body was being wrapped in some sort of energetic linen strips, much like a mummy. The strips were white and were about two inches wide. They began to encircle my mother at her feet and slowly moved up her legs.

I later learned this is a very rare, holy, spirit-world ritual performed on extremely advanced souls who have incarnated many times, learned lots of life lessons, and have had a positive influence on many people's lives. Historians teach about how Egyptian pharaohs and members of their families were wrapped in strips of linen upon their death, and many other religious and spiritual traditions around the world have similarly used burial shrouds—long pieces of cotton or linen wrapped around a body. This ritual is observed in the Jewish, Muslim, and Hindu traditions, and even in practices of some Native American Indian tribes. Many biblical scholars believe Jesus was wrapped in this way after his crucifixion.

The iridescent dry mist I had seen gently swirling in the room (which I now refer to as grace) continued to come and go. At one point, I saw my grandmother holding an infant. *Who could that be?* I wondered. When I mentioned this new development to my sister Joan, she said she thought it might be our cousin Maureen who had drowned in her backyard pool at the age of one and a half. I told my sister that on several occasions I had "seen" Memaw holding Maureen, and Maureen had appeared as a toddler wearing a pink cotton dress with smocking on the chest. (Later, at Mother's funeral, my Aunt Irene, Maureen's mother, told me she had been buried in a pink cotton dress with smocking on the chest.) The infant I saw Memaw holding wasn't Maureen.

I mentioned the baby spirit to my dad and asked if Mother had ever had any miscarriages. He said yes, she did—one, before my older brother Jay was born. I immediately knew that was the infant in Memaw's arms. Since then, I've seen unborn babies' spirits appear around their parents and grandparents countless times.

At about 3 p.m., two angels appeared on either side of the spirit bubble above my mother's head. These angels looked exactly like the rest of the angels surrounding my mother's bed, all of whom I would later come to recognize as guardian angels. They were between six and seven feet tall, with fair complexions and shoulder-length blonde hair that fell in soft waves. They also had huge white wings and wore floor-length white robes that were belted at the waist with a vanilla-colored rope.

An hour later, the wings of these angels began to move with the grace of a giant owl. The tempo was fairly slow and very smooth and it had a rhythmic quality. I had absolutely no idea why the angels' wings were moving, what it symbolized, or for how long this movement would continue. Mother was still incommunicative. At times she appeared restless, and by now her eyes were glazed and she stared past us. It was as if she couldn't focus. The hospice nurses told us that was completely normal.

At this point, when I psychically asked Mother if she needed anything, she said she needed Jay. He and his wife Teri had left for a few hours to attend a wedding. The rest of the family (my dad, younger sister Joan and her husband Regis, my younger brother Jon and his wife Gail, my husband Tim, and son Jonathan) were all still there. Even though the hospice nurses believed it would be several days, perhaps even a week, before my mother would die because she had arrived well hydrated, I wasn't so sure. I called Jay and told him Mother was asking for him. He and Teri arrived back at the hospice facility in less than an hour. This seemed to calm her.

Once Jay arrived, I noticed the moving wings of the guardian angels above Mother's head were creating an upward draft, a vacuum. I could both see and feel it. This vacuum reminded me of a drive-through carwash when the dryer sucks all the water off the car. I also noticed that an energetic hole was opening on top of Mother's head at the spot where her spirit bubble was attached. At the time, I remember wondering if the hole and the vacuum would help lift Mother's spirit out of her body when the time came. The thought of how the movement of the angels' wings on the spiritual plane might cause a physical reaction amazed me, and watching it unfold was extraordinary!

The Final Hours

Waiting for a loved one to die can be a long, exhausting process. You want to stay close by to make sure the patient gets good care, so you're always agonizing over whether to stay or go. After all, what if they die while you're away? You want to be supportive, and yet you need to care for yourself as well. My family was experiencing all of those emotions.

After talking with Mother's nurses, we decided it'd be okay if we all left for a brief dinner. The staff once again assured us that based on their vast experience, Mother would be around for at least a few more days. After dinner, several of us went back to the hospice. In the physical world, Mother looked the same. Her eyes were unfocused and glazed. She was unable to squeeze our hands and couldn't voluntarily move herself.

In the spiritual world however, a lot had changed.

As the day had progressed, the circle of guardian angels had been opening up into various stages of a horseshoe shape, and by this point they had formed a straight line across the room at the foot of the bed. My grandparents' spirits however, had stayed planted at my mother's feet. It had become obvious that my grandmother was running the show from the spirit world perspective. It was she who brought in the angels when the time was right. It was she who summoned the family and friends' spirits to stand guard with her during my mother's last hours on earth. And it was she who monitored the progression of my mother's dying process.

The strips of linen had also been advancing as the day wore on, and by now they were all the way up to Mother's shoulders. In addition, the hole above her head had doubled in size and the vacuum had grown significantly stronger.

By 9 p.m., my family decided to go home to get some sleep and we all agreed to reconvene early the next morning. I, on the other hand, decided to spend the night with my mom in her room. Based on what I was seeing, and in spite of what the nurses were saying, I believed my mother might not last through the night. I told everyone I'd call if anything changed.

I sat holding my mother's hand, told her I loved her, thanked her for everything she'd done for me, and let her know that I'd be spending the night with her. I also told her that everyone in the family would be fine, that we'd take care of Dad, and that we were all okay with her going on to Heaven.

As the evening wore on into night, more and more spirits continued to fill the room. So many spirits had gathered along the sides and at the foot of my mother's bed that they stretched far into the distance and looked like dots on the horizon. It was as if the walls in the hospice room weren't there anymore. It was now just wall-to-wall spirits—belonging to everyone whose life she had ever touched and many more—all there to welcome Mother to Heaven.

By midnight, the strips of linen were wrapped around her entire body. The vacuum above her head was continuing to grow stronger, and it was now obvious to me that the continual slow motion of the angels' wings on either side of my mother's spirit bubble was causing this phenomenon.

Mother rarely opened her eyes, moved, or expressed any emotion. Her skin felt hot. I wondered if she had a fever, maybe from fighting some sort of infection. The nurses told me it was common for a dying person to run a temperature. They explained that as the body begins to shut down, certain areas of the brain no longer function properly—including the part regulating body temperature.

Around 2 a.m., I went to the nurses' station and chatted with the two women on night duty. I asked them what symptoms occur when the end is getting close. They told me the patient's breathing gets very labored and their feet and extremities turn blue. Again, they assured me that based on their observations, my mother would be around for several more days. And again, based on what I was seeing from the spiritual side, I didn't agree.

I dozed off at one point and was awakened around 5:30 a.m. by the sound of my mother's very labored breathing. I raised her bed sheet and saw that her feet were blue.

At that point, I summoned the nurses. After checking her, they agreed the time had come to call the family. They said they'd stay with her until I returned.

I went out into the hallway and called my husband who with our son was staying at my parents' house. I then called my brothers and sister and asked them to come right away. As I returned to the room, I knelt next to my mother's bed and held her right hand. I told her I loved her, that everyone was on their way, and that it was okay if she couldn't hold on until they arrived. The two nurses were on the other side of the bed.

My mother died at 5:50 a.m., about ten minutes before the family arrived. She died holding my hand, looking into my eyes. After Mother took her last breath, one of the nurses listened to her heart and told me she was gone. Although I knew her body was dead, I could see that her spirit had yet to depart.

Still holding her hand, I closed my eyes and watched as the two guardian angels on either side of my mother's "spirit bubble" turned themselves and Mother completely around, before all three flew up in a diagonal direction to the right. I was confident they were escorting her to Heaven. As soon as Mother's spirit left, the other angels and all the spirits of her family and friends as well as her pets faded away.

My Mother's Parting Gift

Needless to say, my mother had given me an exceptional gift by allowing me to see what was happening spiritually as she died. She was the first person with whom I saw the angels and spirits of loved ones gather as she herself approached death. At the end of her funeral, true to the Catholic tradition, the priest said *In Paradisum*, a prayer I'd heard many times before. But now, I really *heard* it for the first time and it really made sense to me in a way it never could have before. *This is what I saw!* I thought. Among other things, the prayer says, "May the angels lead you into Paradise." This is what I saw. "May the martyrs come to welcome you to the Holy City." This is what I saw. "May choirs of angels welcome you and lead you to the bosom of Abraham." That's what I saw.

I realized that whoever wrote that prayer thousands of years ago saw what I saw. They wrote that prayer because it describes what happens when someone dies.

My head was reeling. While I was grieving the loss of my mother, I was simultaneously marveling at everything I'd seen in the past few days—and I was still trying to process it all. Was this a common occurrence? Did everyone have angels and spirits of deceased loved ones with them when they died? I'd heard about dying people telling their families they were seeing deceased relatives, especially parents and spouses. I'd heard of people on their deathbeds seeing angels and sometimes even Jesus or other religious figures. Most of us believe the dying person is somewhat delusional when they see spirits. But maybe they aren't delusional after all.

And what about the animal spirits? What about the circle of angels opening up to make a horseshoe shape and then eventually forming a straight line? Did it always progress in this way as a person approached death? And is there really a hole that opens on top of a person's head where a vacuum forms to help the spirit separate from the body? Is this what people with near-death experiences refer to as "going through the tunnel"? Did I just imagine that the movement of the angels' wings created the vacuum? Did I really see and feel the upward pull that helped my mother's spirit exit from her body?

Now, after years of additional experience, I can definitively say the answer to all those questions is yes. These things really do happen, and they happen for everyone, regardless of how a person dies, what religion the person is, or what beliefs they hold. In the years since my mother's passing, I have worked with many families when one of their loved ones is dying. Each person's death has its own nuances, but everyone goes through the 12 phases of transition as their spirit leaves their body.

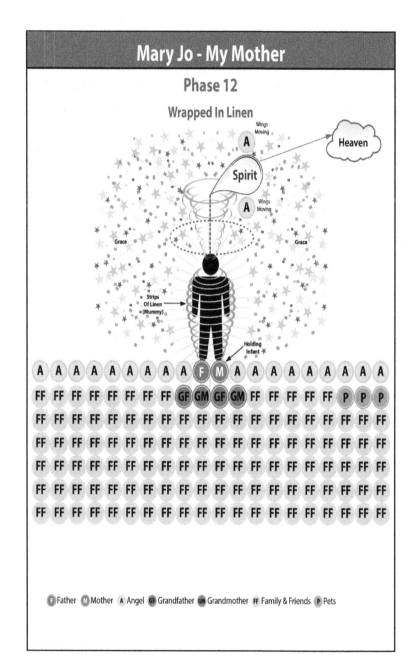

Mary Jo - My Mother

Phase 12

Wrapped In Linen

F Father M Mother A Angel GF Grandfather GM Grandmother FF Family & Friends P Pets

Chapter 3

What to Expect from This Book

$\mathscr{P}$art I of this book has given you the background about how I came to see what I see and to understand what it means. Next, Part II will detail what I've seen and experienced with clients. Within this upcoming section, Chapter 4 will describe in detail each of the 12 phases of transition, with graphics to make it easier for you to picture each phase. Chapter 5 will take you through an experience that I call a "Walk to Heaven," where I lead clients on a dress rehearsal journey to the other side and back to help them lose their fear of what will happen at the moment of transition. Chapter 6 will discuss other occasions when angels and spirits assist us, such as when we're sick or in surgery, with a few interesting examples.

In Part III, I'll share some stories about being with various people when they died (or about scanning them psychically when my help was requested) and the intriguing experiences I've witnessed during that process. In addition, I will also share an unforgettable experience I had while psychically replaying the death of Saint Pope John Paul II (as well as actually and psychically watching what was happening during his funeral). As in Part II, I've included graphics with several of these stories to illustrate unusual scenarios.

My hope is the information I've learned over the past couple of decades as well as the stories I share will bring you to a greater understanding of what happens to us when we make our transitions. May it both comfort you in supporting those you love during their passing as well as reassure you that you, too, will be lovingly escorted to Heaven when the time comes for you to leave the physical world.

Part II

What I See

Chapter 4

The 12 Phases of Transition

When someone asks me to help with a dying person, I first scan the scene in my mind. Based on what I see, I can usually get a pretty good idea of what phase the person is in and how close they are to dying. I always psychically ask the patient three questions:

1) Are you ready to go?
2) Are you in pain?
3) What do you need?

And I always get answers—although those answers typically change throughout the hours and days leading up to death.

What follows are descriptions of each of the phases, along with diagrams to help you picture them. All the graphics are designed to show the dying person lying on their back, face up, so when I describe something being on the right, it refers to the reader's right (the dying person's left) as we look at the diagram.

Phase 1

Spirit Exits The Body

The first thing that happens when someone is dying is their spirit exits the body and remains attached to the top of their head. As I mentioned before, this looks very much like the kind of bubble that comic strip artists draw to show dialogue.

It's important to note that our spirit naturally leaves and re-enters our bodies throughout our lives. In fact, this often happens at night when we have dreams about flying. This is called astral travel, and we can also do it consciously. I have often traveled to remote locations with clients during a session, describing a location that ends up being a place the client recognizes (such as a childhood home, a favorite vacation spot, or a place they frequent). So when this happens to us, it's not always a sign we're dying; however, when we do get ready to exit the earth plane for good, this is the first step.

When you hear about near-death experiences (going through a tunnel toward a bright light) from people who have almost died, it corroborates with what I see with clients. As someone is dying, their spirit starts exiting the body from the feet and works its way up through the top of their head. That's what people see as they go through their own personal tunnel. Once the spirit emerges through the crown chakra on top of the head, it stays attached until the time of actual death. (In yoga philosophy, a chakra is an energy center in the body.)

The Twelve Phases of Transformation™

Phase 1

Spirit Exits Body

Phase 2

Parents Arrive

The second phase is when the spirits of the dying person's parents arrive. It's always the closest maternal spirit to the dying person who appears first, then the spirit of the father immediately follows. If both of the person's parents are still alive, the maternal grandparents will be present. If the person's mother is alive, the deceased father and the dying person's maternal grandmother (their mother's mother) or maternal great grandmother (their mother's grandmother) will appear. If the maternal grandparents are still alive, it'll be the maternal great grandparents who come first. In other words, the closest deceased maternal relatives will be present in Phase 2 and will direct the dying process from the spiritual world for their child or grandchild.

I'm often asked what happens in the case when a person has been adopted. What I see in this situation is the adoptive mother and father (the ones who raised the dying person) and their relatives are the spirits who are in command, while the birth parents are there as observers.

I find it fascinating how the mother (or maternal grandmother or great grandmother) is always the one who runs the show in the spirit world. Mothers not only take care of their children when they're alive, but they also take care of them after their own deaths. The mother is the one who summons the angels as well as the spirits of relatives and friends.

When the dying person has been adopted, the adoptive mother (or her maternal relative) has the spirit-world responsibility.

The maternal spirit is always positioned at the left foot of the person who is dying, while the paternal spirit is always positioned at the right foot. If the person was adopted, the adoptive mother is still at the patient's left foot and the birth mother is to her right. Similarly, the adoptive father remains at the patient's right foot, while the birth father is to his left. It's interesting to note that according to the Kabbalah (ancient Jewish mysticism), the left side of our bodies is the feminine side and relates to feminine characteristics (nurturing, love, domestic responsibilities), while the right side is masculine and represents what we think of as more masculine traits (provider, protector, hunter). It's similar to the right brain/left brain concept. Different sides of our brains represent different skill sets. So in essence, what I see with regard to the placement of the parent spirits (mother at the patient's left foot and father at the patient's right foot) corresponds with these ancient beliefs.

The Twelve Phases of Transformation™

Phase 2

Parents Arrive

F Father M Mother

Phase 3

Angels Arrive

The third phase is when the guardian angels arrive. They're big—six to seven feet tall—and they're each dressed in a white flowing gown. They all have long, blonde hair that falls in soft waves to their shoulders, and they all look the same—in fact, they're unisex.

Keep in mind my description of guardian angels is based on how they appear to me so I can identify them. The picture I see in my mind is based on how I believe angels look and is certainly influenced by my Catholic education.

In reality, angels are just energy and can appear in an endless variety of forms. These guardian angels, along with the parental spirits, form a circle around the dying person's bed. The circle is usually a few feet away from the bed, and the parents are always the anchor. The angels come to facilitate the transition from human (physical) form into purely spiritual (non-physical) form.

The Twelve Phases of Transformation™

Phase 3

Angels Arrive

F Father M Mother A Angel

Phase 4

Angels Form Horseshoe

In the fourth phase, the original circle of angels starts to open and forms a horseshoe shape. The maternal spirit remains totally focused on the dying person, without paying attention to anyone else in the room (human or spirit). These mother spirits always perform with an intensity of focus I've never seen anywhere else. No distraction can interrupt the maternal spirit and her duty to facilitate the spiritual side of the dying process for her loved one. The paternal spirit is still present, too, and lends plenty of support.

Think about your family and the families of friends and relatives. In most cases, it's the mom who organizes meals, car pools, bath time, homework, and so on—the one who makes the family unit operational. From what I repeatedly see, it's also the deceased mothers who organize everything in the spiritual transition process as well.

The Twelve Phases of Transformation™

Phase 4

Angels Form Horseshoe

Spirit

🟤 Father 🔵 Mother Ⓐ Angel

Phase 5

Additional Angels Guard Spirit

In the fifth phase, two additional guardian angels appear on either side of the spirit bubble. They, along with the person's own guardian angel, are perhaps the most important angels in the dying scenario. These two angels are very instrumental in helping the person's spirit leave their body. As you'll see in a later phase, these angels eventually escort the dying person's spirit to Heaven.

Belief in guardian angels dates back to the beginning of recorded history. They're prevalent in the traditions of most cultures, and the Bible and other holy texts are filled with stories about them.

Each of us has a guardian angel assigned to our spirit who guides, advises, protects, and advocates on our behalf. These heavenly representatives arrive the moment our spirits enter our bodies prior to birth. I believe spirits keep the same guardian angel throughout all of their lifetimes. As we're dying, our own guardian angel always stands to the right of the maternal spirit and aids her with the person's transitioning process. It's like the dying person's maternal spirit and guardian angel are the CEO and COO of their customized spiritual adventure back into non-physical.

The Twelve Phases of Transformation™

Phase 5

Additional Angels Guard Spirit

F Father M Mother A Angel

Phase 6

Spirits Arrive

By the start of the sixth phase, the spirits of extended family and friends begin to appear. The two angels are still in position on either side of the spirit bubble, and the horseshoe of angels is now widening. If the dying person's spouse has already passed, that person is located behind and to the right of the mother's spirit. If the person has more than one deceased spouse, all of them line up in this position, with the most recent spouse located closest to the mother's spirit. The next most recent spouse would be to the right of the first spouse, and so on. I believe all of these family spirits serve as a type of "Welcome to Heaven" committee.

Interestingly enough, immediate family, family of origin, and very close friends from this lifetime stand in the front row behind the angels and the person's parents. Behind them are other family and friends from this lifetime. Behind them stand family, friends, and other spirits from many lifetimes. Every spirit present has had some connection to the dying person in one of their lives and is now participating in their transition from this human lifetime into the purely spiritual (non-physical) form.

The Twelve Phases of Transformation™

Phase 6

Spirits Arrive

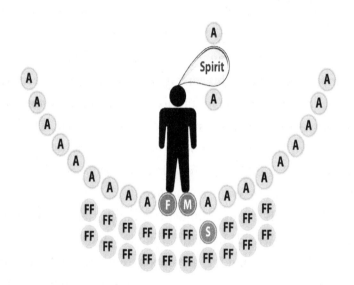

F Father M Mother A Angel S Spouse FF Family & Friends

Phase 7

Animal Spirits Arrive

In the seventh phase, animal spirits arrive. These are the spirits of all the pets the person has had during this lifetime and they're always grouped to the right of the person's bed. This pet zone may include any kind of animal. Over the years, I've seen not only dogs and cats but also horses, cows, chickens, rabbits, snakes, lambs, and goats, among other species. They all stand or sit at attention, and they're very well behaved. It's as if they're a type of honor guard.

When I describe the pet spirits I'm seeing to the family, they can often identify the animal by name.

More than half of all American households have a pet, and most people think of their pets as a member of the family, so it makes sense their spirits would be present. Our pets provide unconditional love, they're always happy to see us, they guard and protect us, and they comfort us in times of sadness. Research shows having a pet can lead to a better quality of life. People with pets generally have healthier hearts, are less sick and depressed, and get more exercise than those without a pet.

In this phase, the horseshoe of parents and angels continues to widen, and more family and friends' spirits continue to arrive.

The Twelve Phases of Transformation™

Phase 7

Animal Spirits Arrive

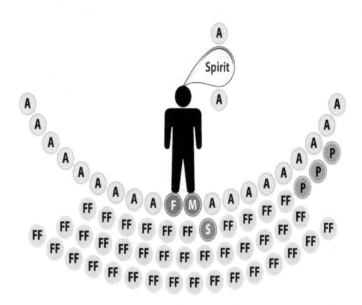

Father Mother Angel Spouse FF Family & Friends Pets

Phase 8

Horseshoe Expands

The horseshoe of angels and parents continues to widen in the eighth phase. This widening is to expand the line of demarcation between the human (physical) and the spirit world (non-physical) realities.

Everything else looks the same as before in this phase. The spirit bubble is still attached to and floating above the dying person's head, family and friends' spirits are still in place, and the pet zone is still intact.

The Twelve Phases of Transformation™

Phase 8

Horseshoe Expands

F Father M Mother A Angel S Spouse FF Family & Friends P Pets

Phase 9

Many Spirits Arrive

When I see many spirits in the room, I know the person has reached the ninth phase and is approaching death. These spirits look like regular people to me. They're both male and female, and they're all ages, sizes, and nationalities. They're from many different times and cultures and they appear in period dress. I've seen them in clothing from ancient times, medieval days, the Victorian era, and throughout the 20th and 21st centuries. For example, Native Americans often appear in clothing made out of animal skins decorated with beading and feathers. I've even seen Native American male spirits appear in the full feathered headdress reserved only for the chief of the tribe. All spirits appear in a form that can be recognized by me so I may convey their presence to the family.

Oftentimes, when I describe the appearance of a spirit to the dying person or to one of their family members, they can almost always identify that spirit. Sometimes I'm shown photographs of the family member or friend I'm describing. When I acknowledge that particular spirit is present, it normally ends up comforting the family.

The Twelve Phases of Transformation™

Phase 9

Many Spirits Arrive

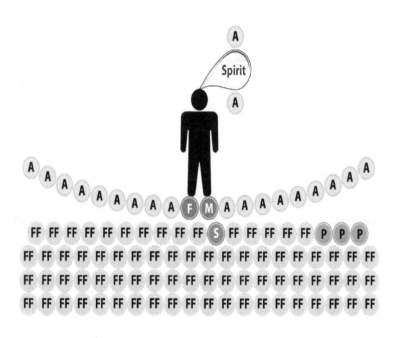

F Father M Mother A Angel S Spouse FF Family & Friends P Pets

Phase 10

Vacuum Forms and Hole Opens

In the tenth phase, the horseshoe continues to open up. It's now almost a straight line, and I see the wings of the two angels on either side of the spirit bubble start to move. At the same time, an opening begins to appear above the patient's head. That's when I know death is close.

The movement of the angels' wings creates an opening in the crown chakra on top of the head and produces a vacuum above it that helps the spirit separate from the body. The vacuum is similar to those you see in drive-through car washes that suck the water off your car right before you exit. This spiritual vacuum has a physical sensation for me—I not only see it, I can feel and hear it too.

The angels' wings move at a constant, fairly slow speed, much like an owl's wings. (Owls can move their wings more slowly and silently than other birds, and interestingly, the owl signifies death in numerous traditions all over the world.)

The moving wings of the angels not only create lift but also cause a vortex or vacuum to form. (I found it interesting to learn that when a bird flaps its wings, it creates something called a wingtip vortex, a circular pattern of rotating air left behind a wing as it generates lift; this happens because the faster-moving air going over the top of the wing exerts less pressure than the slower-moving air underneath the wing.)

The vortex/vacuum resulting from the movement of the angels' wings is also similar to the funnel cloud of a tornado which sucks up anything in its path. This vacuum is key because it helps the person's spirit detach from their body.

What amazes me the most are the similarities between angels, birds, and even airplanes. The fact that an angelic maneuver in the spirit world actually causes an effect in the person's physical reality is extraordinary to me. I guess it's all just energy.

The Twelve Phases of Transformation™

Phase 10

Vacuum Forms and Hole Opens

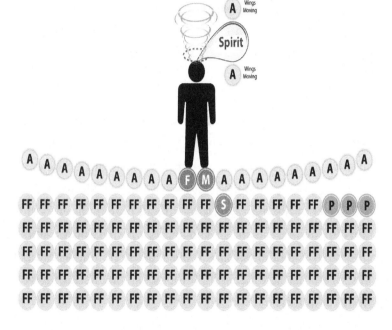

F Father   M Mother   A Angel   S Spouse   FF Family & Friends   P Pets

Phase 11

Angels Form Line

In the eleventh phase, the angels' wings keep moving as the opening at the top of the head continues to expand and the vortex increases in strength. The opening starts out small, maybe just a few inches wide, and can eventually grow to as much as several feet on either side of the person's head. As this hole opens wider, the upward pull becomes increasingly more intense.

By this phase, the guardian angels and parents are in a straight line at the foot of the bed. I think of this as angelic crowd control. It's the line of demarcation between the non-physical spirit world and our physical reality. The caregivers—the nurses and the doctors as well as the living family and friends of the dying person—are all on the patient's side of this line, while the angels and spirits which by now number in the hundreds (and perhaps thousands, stretching as far as I can see) are on the other side. It looks like one heck of a welcoming committee.

This is exactly what *In Paradisum* describes. The prayer talks about how the angels and our departed loved ones are going to greet us and lead us into paradise. I personally find this very comforting, and so do the families of dying people with whom I've worked. It seems to help take some of the fear out of the whole death and dying process.

The Twelve Phases of Transformation™

Phase 11

Angels Form Line

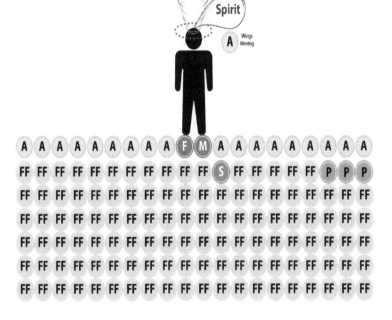

F Father M Mother A Angel S Spouse FF Family & Friends P Pets

Phase 12

Spirit to Heaven

Phase 12 is the final phase—the grand exit. By this point, the vacuum has become powerful enough to lift the spirit completely out of the body (at which point the spirit no longer looks like a bubble and instead resembles a hologram of a complete human form).

As the spirit emerges through the crown chakra on top of the head and disconnects from the body, it and its two angelic escorts are all facing frontwards.

Once it's out, the spirit and its escort angels turn 180 degrees, face the opposite direction and go up into the light, to Heaven.

The person's spirit is always taken up and to the right, as I'm looking at the scene. It's interesting to note that if you look at death scenes in the old masters' paintings, the spirit is always going up and to the right. I believe this is more confirmation that throughout history, others have witnessed what I see.

Once the spirit and angels depart, I'm always filled with an overwhelming sense of peace.

The Twelve Phases of Transformation™

Phase 12

Spirit To Heaven

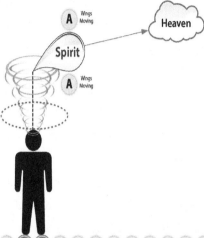

A A A A A A A A A F M A A A A A A A A A
FF FF FF FF FF FF FF FF FF FF FF S FF FF FF FF FF P P P
FF FF FF FF FF FF FF FF FF FF FF FF FF FF FF FF FF FF FF FF
FF FF FF FF FF FF FF FF FF FF FF FF FF FF FF FF FF FF FF FF
FF FF FF FF FF FF FF FF FF FF FF FF FF FF FF FF FF FF FF FF
FF FF FF FF FF FF FF FF FF FF FF FF FF FF FF FF FF FF FF FF
FF FF FF FF FF FF FF FF FF FF FF FF FF FF FF FF FF FF FF FF

F Father M Mother A Angel S Spouse FF Family & Friends P Pets

No One Dies Alone

Many people find it extremely comforting to know that none of us truly dies alone. This can be particularly reassuring for the family and friends of those who die unexpectedly without being surrounded by human love and support. The truth is, there's a huge crowd of spirit entities gathered at every death to assist the dying person with their transition and to escort them to the non-physical next world—Heaven.

How Long Do the 12 Phases Take?

Even though this sequence is always the same for everyone, the rate of progression can vary. These phases can be instantaneous or they can stretch out over many months or even years. Most people go through the phases in anywhere from a few hours to a few days. The guardian angels and the spirits of family members are there whether a person has a drawn-out dying process or whether they die quite suddenly, including if they die in an accident, disaster, homicide, or suicide. In such cases, the angels and spirits may have been in position for weeks—or the person could go through all the phases in their complete fullness in what we experience here on the physical plane as a nanosecond. After all, the linear way we experience time is not necessarily how time is calculated in other realms.

No matter how long it appears to take, all 12 of these phases happen to all humans. Each person's dying process has nuances that pertain specifically to that person.Some of the differences are quite extraordinary, while others are subtle.

All are glorious!

Do Bad People Get Angelic Escorts?

This assistance happens for *everyone,* regardless of whether society labels them as a good person or not—and I assure you the process for each person is really very holy. After all, everyone's spirit is pure energy, pure light, and pure goodness—even a mass murderer's spirit. When a person's spirit leaves the body, all the negative emotions and behavior of the human experience stay with that human body.

What Does the Dying Person See?

In most instances, I've found that the dying person is aware of the spiritual happenings going on in the room. I believe this is true even if they are non-communicative. Hospice workers often explain to family members that it's completely normal, and to be expected, for the dying person to talk about seeing deceased loved ones and angels—or sometimes even a religious figure like Jesus, Buddha, or Krishna.

I believe as people hover between life and death, they're in somewhat of a middle ground between two realities (the physical and non-physical). This enables them while they're still alive to begin to perceive the spirit world. I also believe we all have the ability to witness psychic phenomena. Most of us shut off these abilities if we're repeatedly told as children what we're seeing isn't real, or that it's just our imagination. Parents who, on the other hand, validate their children when they witness psychic phenomena are doing their children a great service.

I somehow knew this even before I was aware I was psychic. As a baby, my son Jonathan was highly verbal. He talked in complete sentences before he could walk. Every night, he'd fall asleep in my arms while drinking his bottle, being rocked in the glider chair, and listening to me sing to him.

On several occasions, he abruptly sat up, pointed to a corner of the ceiling in his bedroom and said, "What's that?"

"What do you see?" I'd ask.

"A big red ball," he'd say.

"Oh, that's just energy," I'd answer. My explanation always seemed to satisfy him.

Even though I couldn't see the big red ball of energy, he obviously could, and I instinctively knew I needed to validate what he said he saw. When we acknowledge our children's observations of psychic phenomena and encourage them to hone this ability, they will eventually learn to use this skill in service to themselves and to others.

Can the Dying Person Hear & Understand Me?

Absolutely! From what I've witnessed both in person and psychically, the dying person knows exactly who is with them, what they're saying, and what they need to transition into the spirit world. That's why it's important to tell your dying relative/friend anything that is important to you or anything you believe could be important to them. Although most of us want to spare our dying loved one from having to listen to conversations with medical professionals, whether or not you're in their room, outside in the hallway, or in a conference room, your relative/friend knows what is being said. Likewise, I believe we all have control over when we die and who's present at the time of death.

Do All Angels Look Like That?

It's vital to underscore the reason I see blonde, Caucasian angels dressed in long white robes is my frame of reference is based on a Catholic School education that came with millennia of paintings depicting angels in this manner. Does that mean it's what angels *really* look like? No!

I'm sure other psychics have their own interpretation of how angels (or beings like angels) appear. I think that's how they appear to me so I can recognize them for the types of beings they are. I firmly believe intuitives with other religious backgrounds who witness a deathbed scene will see beings that make sense within their tradition or frame of reference—whether that is Buddhist, Muslim, Native American, Hindu, Judeo-Christian, and so on.

In reality, spiritual entities are just energy. Because angels aren't physical, they don't truly have human-like characteristics. They just *appear* a certain way to us because it's what we expect and what we understand.

I find being able to see these entities in this familiar way and to describe them to others is profoundly comforting for them and extremely humbling for me.

Chapter 5

A Walk to Heaven

The vast majority of people with whom I work (including clients' loved ones who they ask me to scan) are afraid to die. They're scared about the whole process of what will happen at the time of death. So I often take them—psychically—on what I call a "Walk to Heaven." This is a kind of dress rehearsal so they'll know what to expect when their spirit separates from their body. I reassure them psychically that I will be with them the whole time during our walk, and that seeing this fascinating process will help to alleviate their fears. Although some people are initially afraid to take this meditative journey, so far, everyone I have suggested this to has agreed to take the "walk" with me. Here's how it goes:

Sacred Sands

I separate my spirit from my body. It exits through the crown chakra on the top of my head just like a spirit does when someone is dying. Then my spirit instantly joins my client's spirit and our spirits walk through the desert into a setting sun that's a mix of brilliant oranges and yellows.

The core is a somewhat deeper orange (the color of a tangerine), which lightens in hue closer to the edge. (Imagine the color of a tangerine blending into the color of a navel orange, which then blends into the color of orange juice, which then blends into the color of lemonade.) The sun grows in size as we get closer and closer to it.

We are both barefoot, we can feel the warm sand between our toes, and we can see the line of sand separated by our strides. The sand is dry and soft, so we don't leave footprints—just a small trough in the sand as we pass through the desert. No one else is around; it's just the two of us in a wide-open space as far as the eye can see. No trees or vegetation are present, and we don't see any animals or insects.

The sky is a pale blue with white puffy clouds. As we near the sunset, although the light is intense, it's not painful to look at it. We can feel the sun's warmth increase as we draw nearer to it, yet it never feels uncomfortably hot. We are both silent as we walk. All we can hear is our footsteps as we advance through the sand.

Into the Sun

When we reach the sun, we walk right into it. As we do, we hear popping noises all around. It sort of reminds me of how popcorn sounds in an air popper. The sun feels comfortably warm as we pass through it, like getting into a bed heated by an electric blanket on a cold winter's night, or standing in the sun on the first warm day of spring.

As we walk through the setting sun, we eventually come

to a silent black void. It reminds me of those wormholes from science fiction movies—like in the Jodie Foster movie *Contact*. (By the way, wormholes are often described as hypothetical tunnel-like features of space-time that provide a kind of shortcut between two separate points.)

The temperature remains comfortable, and we keep walking forward. It feels as if we're walking on air because we can't feel anything on the bottom of our feet or anywhere on our bodies. There are no sounds, sights, or other physical sensations. We spend a few seconds in this black void. Then all of a sudden we emerge and come upon a wall of resplendent yellow-white light. It is blindingly brilliant, yet not at all uncomfortable to see. The wall stretches as far vertically and horizontally as the eye can see, without any visible way to get around it.

We walk straight through this wall of light, which has a rubbery, plasma-like consistency that easily allows us to pass. When we arrive on the other side, the opening we made as we walked through immediately closes without a trace. Now, we stay stationary. In the distance, we see many spirits of family and friends (including those who may be currently also present at the dying person's bedside).

"Welcome to Heaven" Committee

These spirits, unlike those who appear in period dress in the room of a dying person, are all clothed in long, white cotton gowns with long sleeves (like the gown an altar boy or girl wears). Who we see depends on whether the client's parents are deceased. If the mother is deceased, she is standing in front of the group. If the mother is still alive and the father is deceased, he is in front. If both parents are still living, the maternal grandmother heads the group. If she's still living, the maternal grandfather does the duty.

It's very common to see the spirit out front holding one or more infant spirits—usually babies who have died either in utero or shortly after being born. They can be the dying person's children, grandchildren, or siblings. I recently saw a father's spirit holding three infants' spirits in his arms. The daughter of the dying woman told me her mother had three siblings who died as infants. Babies identified.

All of these spirits are part of the "Welcome to Heaven" committee.

Once the person sees their deceased family and friends, we turn around and go back through the plasma-like wall of light, back through the black void, back through the setting sun, and back through the desert. The client's spirit reattaches to the head of their body and I put my spirit back into my own body.

After the Journey

After the walk is completed, I tell the dying person (psychically) that this is what will happen when it's their time to go. I continue to remind them of our walk each time I scan them during their dying process. Some people lose all their fear on the first trip. If the person is very afraid of death, I'll repeat this exercise with them several times during the dying process. On subsequent walks, as the individual gets closer to death, the group of family and friends will move closer to us once we're on the other side of the heavenly wall of light.

Dying people who are tremendously afraid gain confidence each time we complete the journey. I find their fear can emanate from religious beliefs about souls suffering in Purgatory or even Hell. When people witness what is to come, their fear abates. It's marvelous for me to see the sense of relief, peace, and sometimes even anticipation for the spiritual journey ahead that individuals gain through this exercise.

One person I helped was a nun—someone you wouldn't imagine would be afraid to die, yet she required several walks to Heaven. On the first one, she appeared as her 90-year-old self and used a walker. As we progressed through the desert, setting sun, black void, and plasma wall into Heaven, she hunched over her walker and moved at a very slow pace. On the second trip, she was still hunched over her walker but seemed to move a little quicker. On the way back from the third trip, she flung her walker over her shoulder, stood upright and walked at a rapid pace. After three trips, she knew how close her family and friends were on the other side of the brilliant wall of light and her fear totally vanished.

Chapter 6

Additional Angelic Assistance

*A*ngels don't appear or present themselves only when people are clearly dying. They arrive whenever there's a chance that something big could go wrong—for example, when a person is very sick, under anesthesia in surgery, or near death (even if they're not actually going to die). The guardian angels and spirits are present "just in case" anytime a risk or serious danger is possible. In some instances, I believe guardian angels can even prevent something bad or life-threatening from happening. Many of us have heard stories of a person magically appearing to shield someone from a car about to hit them or protect them from some other tragedy occurring. In most of those instances, a person/entity seems to appear out of nowhere and then vanishes as quickly as they came.

I'm often asked to scan people remotely when they're having surgery. What I see is similar to what I see when someone is dying, with a few key differences. First, the patient's guardian angel is always floating above the anesthesiologist's (or nurse anesthetist's) head. And second, one or more surgeon spirits are floating above the actual surgeon or surgeons performing the operation. In addition to these spirit beings, I can see the human doctors and nurses quite clearly as they work, and oftentimes I can even read the numbers on the various anesthesia monitors.

I scanned my sister-in-law Wyanda a few years ago while she was having surgery in another state. A few days after she got home, I relayed what I had seen take place during her operation. She wanted to know what spirits were in the room, and especially if her deceased mother was present (she was). During the conversation, I mentioned that I saw three surgeons operating on her along with three surgeon spirits floating over them, acting as advisors. Wyanda was insistent that only two surgeons were present.

"Well, I saw three," I told her, "but maybe I'm wrong." A few weeks later, she called to tell me I was right—her medical bills clearly listed the three surgeons who had performed her operation!

Similar to when people are dying, spirits of deceased family, friends, and others stand in a horseshoe formation at the foot of the operating table. Similar to the Twelve Phases of Transition when a person is dying, the patient's closest deceased female maternal relative (mother, maternal grandmother, maternal great grandmother, and so on) and father (if he is deceased) or the closest deceased male maternal relative (maternal grandfather, maternal great grandfather, and so on) are present. In the surgery configuration however, the maternal spirit is at the patient's right foot and the paternal spirit is at the patient's left foot. It's the opposite of the parents' spirits positions when someone is dying. In addition, several lines of deceased family members, friends, and others' spirits may form several rows, one behind the other, in the horseshoe pattern at the foot of the operating table.

A correlation usually exists between how much prayer is being said for the patient and how many spirits are in the operating room lending support. When I see a lot of spirits in the room, I know many people are praying for that patient. After all, prayer is a way of focusing energy and when a group of us are focused on a common situation/goal, it can have a profound effect.

A couple years ago my friend Sharrie Jones Viar's daughter Leah had surgery. While scanning her, I saw the normal scenario with her guardian angel floating above the head of the anesthesiologist, the doctor spirits floating over the heads of the surgeons, and lots of family and friends' spirits standing in a horseshoe formation at the foot of the operating table. I drew the scene on a piece of paper and gave it to Leah a few days later when I saw her in person. As I was describing my drawing to her, I told her that based on the number of spirits I saw in the operating room, she must have had a lot of people praying for her. Leah told me that couldn't be accurate because only a handful of people even knew she was having surgery.

Her mother then asked if Leah's son (who was 10 years old) could've possibly asked his friends at Summer Bible Camp to pray for her. Leah then realized her son had in fact mentioned he had asked his camp to pray for his mom on the morning of her surgery. Mystery solved.

I don't normally see a person's spirit bubble during surgery (as I do when someone is dying) because the patient is not yet making their transition. If, however, they run into problems and a serious threat to their health develops, I often see a circle of angels surrounding the operating table.

I want to make it clear the angels and spirits, no matter the number, are there for emotional support. The success of the surgery doesn't depend on their intervention. It is affected by the patient's free will and by how the outcome of the surgery is meant to play into the patient's life story from a much broader viewpoint. After all, each of us has a purpose and a life path with many adventures to experience.

The "Just in Case" Scenario

About 12 years ago, my husband Tim had arthroscopic surgery on his knee to repair a torn meniscus. I was in pre-op with him until just before the surgery. He was fine. His vital signs (blood pressure, pulse, and so on) were all normal and he was in good spirits. I kissed him good-bye and told him I loved him when they came to take him to surgery. Then I proceeded to the family waiting room.

Once I was settled, I scanned Tim in the operating room and saw the normal scenario. Tim's guardian angel was floating above the anesthesiologist and two surgeon spirits were floating over the head of the surgeon performing the operation. Tim's mother's spirit was at his right foot (the usual position for surgery), and since his father was still alive, his maternal grandfather's spirit was at his left foot. Tim's maternal grandmother was next to his mother, and his paternal grandparents were next to his maternal grandfather. Other spirits were next to them on both sides, and still more were behind them in three more horseshoe-shaped rows like a mini amphitheater at the foot of the operating table. Because this is what I'm used to seeing in surgery, none of this seemed out of the ordinary .

I also saw angels surrounding Tim in the horseshoe position except unlike the death scene, this horseshoe of angels was at his head and extended to his shoulders. At first, I thought I was imagining this, but after several more scans, I knew what I was seeing was correct. I wondered why the angels were present and the significance of this new configuration. After all, this was just a knee scope and Tim's spirit was still in his body—there wasn't a spirit bubble over his head. During the surgery, I received several text updates on Tim's condition from a medical rep friend who was in the operating room with him. Each report said he was doing well, so I dismissed my concern and figured the angels were there with the other spirits to offer their support.

The staff informed me when Tim was out of surgery and had been taken to the recovery room, and they told me I could see him in about an hour. After two hours had elapsed, I was still in the waiting room and hadn't yet been permitted to see him. I asked the person at the information desk several times to find out how much longer I had to wait before I could go back to be with my husband. Each time the reply was that they didn't know.

Finally, after two and a half hours, I was allowed to join Tim and discovered the reason for the long delay. It seems that while he was in the recovery room, Tim had aspirated. Pulmonary aspiration is when a person inhales food, drink, or stomach contents. If this happens while someone is eating, they will either choke or have a coughing fit (often people will say "something went down the wrong pipe"). When it happens during or after surgery, since anesthesia has impaired the gag reflex, pulmonary aspiration can (in the worst cases) result in death by asphyxiation. This is why patients are not allowed to eat or drink for several hours prior to surgery.

By the time I reached Tim's room, several nurses and medical technicians were attending to him. Shortly after I arrived, his surgeon walked into the room saying, "Man, you really gave us a scare!" We learned that when Tim had aspirated in recovery, the staff had suctioned out his lungs. Once he was stabilized, they sent him to radiology for x-rays to be sure his lungs were clear. Of course, Tim didn't remember any of this.

Upon hearing all that had transpired, I realized why the circle of angels was surrounding my husband in the operating room. They were there to protect him—and to assist just in case Tim didn't survive.

Coal Dust in the OR

Several years ago, I was asked to scan a woman who was

having back surgery in San Francisco. Her husband and I chatted several times throughout what ended up being a six-hour procedure. As I scanned the operating room, I saw the same familiar formation: the patient's guardian angel was floating above the head of the anesthesiologist, and two spirit-surgeons were floating above the heads of the human surgeons performing the operation. The patient's parents (both deceased) were at the foot of the operating table, and many other spirits from several generations of the patient's family were also in the room. But oddly, many of these spirits looked dirty, as if they were covered in soot. They reminded me of chimney sweeps in the Mary Poppins movie.

When I told her husband about what I was seeing, he said, "Well, several generations of her family were coal miners in West Virginia." I was seeing spirits covered in coal dust! They appeared that way so I could tell the family, who would then realize these spirits were deceased relatives.

After the surgery, a grandmotherly spirit with her white hair in a bun appeared next to the patient's bed. She was wearing a housedress from the 1940s with an apron over it. Since the husband didn't recognize my description, he called his wife's sister, who identified the woman as "Grandma Anne," the patient's maternal grandmother. Grandma Anne was with the patient in surgery, in the recovery room, and in her hospital room—and she was still with the patient when she went home. Most of the time, deceased family members are with a patient when they're having surgery. These deceased relatives are there to watch over, support, and send love to the patient.

Part III

Transition Stories

Chapter 7

Licorice for Louie

Louie DiSabato, my friend Tracy DiSabato-Aust's father, lingered for months. He had Alzheimer's and had been incommunicative for a long time. As he approached death, I began asking him psychically if he was ready to go, but he kept saying no. When I'd ask him what he needed, he'd say that he needed to say goodbye. It just so happened that all of his family, including his grandchildren, were coming in a few weeks for Christmas. Somehow, he understood that and wanted to wait until he got to see all of them.

Each time I scanned him, I continued to ask Louie if he needed anything else. One day, he said, "Yeah, tell Tracy to bring me some licorice the next time she comes." So I called Tracy and relayed her father's request.

"That's his favorite candy!" she said, bursting out laughing. That was certainly news to me. Tracy dutifully brought her father the licorice.

In mid-January, after Louie had seen all of his family at Christmas, I asked again, "Louie, you ready to go?" The angels and his parents were in the straight line, and the vacuum above his head was strong. He seemed pretty close to me.

"Yeah," he responded. "I'm ready to go now." I asked if he needed anything, and he said, "Yeah. I need clearance."

"What do you mean you need clearance?" I asked, confused. "For what? From whom?" He went on to explain that Heaven had a form of what we know as air traffic control. I had never heard that before. "Heaven has air traffic control?" I asked incredulously.

"Yeah," Louie answered. "I'm just waiting for clearance." He was a character to the very end.

A couple weeks later, Louie must have gotten clearance because he died. A week after his death, I did an instant replay of the time he actually died so I could tell Tracy about it. I heard one of the guardian angels beside his spirit bubble say, "Okay, we've got clearance, are you ready?"

And then I heard Louie answer, "Let's go."

Observations

Louie was by himself when he died. His family had all said their goodbyes and had left town. How often does that happen? A lot. My grandmother did the same thing when she died on New Year's Eve in 2001. I'd just fed Memaw dinner—she ate everything on her plate and even drank a cup of coffee. I told her I'd be back in the morning before catching a plane home. I kissed her goodbye and we each told the other we loved them. Soon after I left, my sister Joan and her husband Regis stopped by and spent about 30 minutes with her.

An hour later, while I was having dinner with my parents

at their home, we got a call from the hospital saying Mem had died. It was surreal. She waited until everyone was gone before she left. She was just six weeks shy of turning 100, and interestingly enough, she had always said she didn't want to see her 100th birthday. For more than 20 years, one of her nightly prayers was to die in her sleep. God granted her both wishes!

Sometimes I believe our loved ones think it's going to be too painful for us to watch them die. I was the only one with my mom when she passed. I told her, "Everybody's on their way. If you want to wait until they get here, that's fine. If you don't, it's okay, I'm here." She died ten minutes before the rest of the family arrived. Most funeral home directors tell stories about people waiting either until they're alone or until the people they need with them are present before they die. Because of experiences like these, I believe people really do have control over when they make their transition.

From Tracy:

Julie, more than anyone else, helped comfort me during my father's long battle. Her insight brought me peace and helped me connect with his needs at a higher level than I thought was possible. It was incredible to hear that my father wanted me to bring him licorice, as Julie had no idea of his sweet tooth. It brought much needed levity to what was otherwise a very sad situation. I find Julie's intuitiveness to be a great gift, which she so unselfishly shares to help others. She is a gift to me and to all those she touches.

Chapter 8

Miss Rose and the Rosary

Rose Maggio was a tiny lady who seemed at first glance to be meek and mild, yet like most first generation Italian-Americans, she was actually anything but. Her daughter and only child, Jo Marie Maggio Parker, is a friend of mine, so I knew Miss Rose well. She was a devoted wife, mother, and grandmother who had gained much wisdom from her many life experiences. She was a southern belle through and through, hence the use of the title "Miss" before her name. Good manners, proper etiquette, and knowing right from wrong were all principles Miss Rose lived by, and she expected those close to her to do the same.

Even though Miss Rose was conservative in most aspects of her life, she was very open to having me scan her and share my findings when she wasn't feeling well. She, Jo Marie, and I had several discussions throughout the years, not only about what I saw when scanning her, but also about how I was able to do this. In particular, she was fascinated with what happened to people when they died. The three of us would chat away on the couch in Miss Rose's living room, and before any of us knew it, an hour had passed.

Regardless of how religious or devout someone is, I often find they become afraid when they're faced with their own mortality. In Miss Rose's case, she seemed more curious than afraid, perhaps because she was an old-school Italian Catholic. Her home and garden were virtually overflowing with Virgin Mary statues, crucifixes, and pictures of saints. Her belief in Heaven was solid.

During the last year of her life, Miss Rose seemed to be in and out of the hospital almost monthly. She became very frail. About five months before she died, I began seeing the Phase 1 scenario. Miss Rose's spirit was out of her body, hovering above her head in the bubble configuration. She stayed in Phase 1 for months, which told me she was preparing to die and that it could be a while before she actually departed.

Over the next few months, as Miss Rose went in and out of the hospital and as her condition weakened, she slowly progressed through the next several phases of transition. Her parents' spirits appeared at her feet and served as the anchors to the circle of guardian angels around her. Her husband's spirit showed up, positioned diagonally to the right behind her mother's spirit, and the dog pound (the animal spirit section) was full. I recognized one dog in particular, a beagle named Dusty who had died about six months before. Miss Rose loved her dogs, and Dusty was perhaps her favorite of all.

As she reached Phase 11, a double line of angels had formed at the foot of her bed. It was as if she needed extra crowd control with the assembling spirits who had joined her welcoming committee to Heaven.

Although she was now unable to communicate verbally, I was able to talk with her psychically. Each time I scanned her, I'd ask Miss Rose if she was ready to go, and she'd say, "No. Not yet." My sense was since Jo Marie was her only child, Miss Rose was reluctant to leave her daughter. Jo Marie was a later-in-life baby whose parents were married 19 years before she was born, so they thought she was the most special, precious child to ever walk the earth.

Throughout the next few days, every time I'd ask if she was ready to go, Miss Rose would tell me no. "Are you afraid you won't go to Heaven?" I asked.

"No," came the answer. "I *know* I'm going to Heaven." (This little lady could be very forceful when necessary.)

"Are you afraid at all?" I asked.

"Yes," she answered. When I asked what she was afraid of, she said she was afraid to leave Jo Marie alone.

"Well, you know, she's not going to be alone, because she has Kim [her husband], and Brandon [her son], and her family, and lots of friends," I reminded her.

"It's not the same," Miss Rose replied. Jo Marie's father died when she was only 21, so I'm sure Miss Rose felt an extra sense of responsibility toward her daughter.

"I know you love her and I know you want to protect her," I said next. "But I promise you, she's going to be fine. After all," I joked, "you're not that strong anymore anyway." She laughed. "Can you watch over her from Heaven?" I asked, and she replied that she indeed would be able to. When I asked if she was in pain and if she needed anything, she answered no to both questions.

Four days later, on a Monday night at about 6:00 p.m., my cell phone rang. It was Jo Marie's husband, Kim. "Can you scan Nana?" he asked, using his name for Miss Rose. At this point, she was at St. Vincent's Hospital in Birmingham. I asked if he wanted me to come to the hospital, but he said he didn't think there would be time—she was about to slip away. I agreed to scan her, and he handed the phone to Jo Marie.

This time, when I asked Miss Rose if she was ready to go, she said yes. I asked if she was in pain, and she said no.

"Ask her if she knows I'll be fine," Jo Marie requested. I did, and Miss Rose answered yes. Maybe she'd had several days to get enough confirmation to know Jo Marie was going to be okay. "Ask her to watch over us from Heaven," Jo Marie requested.

"I will," her mother told me to relay. "I'll always be with you, don't worry." Then Jo Marie wanted me to ask her mother to send a sign that she was all right once she got to Heaven. Miss Rose agreed to do so.

"Miss Rose, do you need anything?" I asked.

"Yes, I want you all to pray," she told me. Jo Marie asked if her mother wanted the family to say any particular prayer and Miss Rose requested they say the Rosary. The Rosary is a sequence of prayers dating back to the 12th century that uses a string of beads to aid in reciting the prayers in a specific order. The prayers that make up the Rosary are divided into different segments, referred to as mysteries, representing events in the lives of Jesus and his mother Mary. Jo Marie asked which mystery her mother wanted them to pray, and Miss Rose indicated she wanted them to pray the Joyful Mysteries.

The family immediately began to pray the Rosary, and Miss Rose died a bit later that evening. When I did a replay of the time of Miss Rose's death, I was fascinated with how large the vortex above her head had become. The vacuum to get her spirit out her body stretched three feet horizontally from the top of her head. It was massive! I've seen 250-pound men have one that's just a little bigger than the circumference of their heads. But apparently, all 85 pounds of Miss Rose required an enormous amount of suction to separate her spirit from her body. Once Miss Rose's spirit disconnected from her body, the two guardian angels on either side of her spirit turned her around and escorted her up and to the right to Heaven.

Observations

The morning after Miss Rose died, something led me to look up on the internet how to pray the Rosary.

As a Catholic, of course I know the basics of how to say the Rosary, but I wasn't indoctrinated in it the way my parents and grandparents were. Although I attended 12 years of Catholic school, I was in the first wave of post-Vatican II students and therefore didn't receive the traditional religious education my older family members did.

What I discovered really intrigued me. I knew the prayers were divided into four sets known as the Mysteries of the

Rosary: Joyful, Luminous, Sorrowful, and Glorious. I also knew that each set had five prayers, making a total of 20 prayers in all. What I didn't know until I did this research was that each mystery is said on a specific day of the week. The prayers assigned to Monday, the day Miss Rose died, just happened to be the Joyful Mysteries—the prayers Miss Rose requested her family say earlier that day.

There's more. The date Miss Rose died happened to be May 2nd. In the Catholic Church, May is considered to be the month of the Virgin Mary, and the prayer dedicated to her is the Rosary. So on some level, even though she was unconscious, Miss Rose knew it was a Monday in May, and that it would be appropriate to pray the Joyful Mysteries of the Rosary on that day. As she was dying, she was able to communicate her specific prayer wishes through me to her family. I found that to be remarkable.

Later in the day, when Jo Marie and her family took a break from making funeral arrangements, I got a chance to talk with her. After asking how she was holding up, I said, "Jo Marie, per your request, your mother has sent you a sign she's okay and in Heaven." I then proceeded to tell her what I'd learned while researching the praying of the Rosary. She was indeed touched and relieved.

It was such a delight to know Miss Rose and to be able to participate in her passing. She remained steadfast in her devotion to her Catholic faith throughout her life—right up until her final breath. Her faith gave her comfort, peace, and the ability to accept her death without fear. Her only hesitation was one I believe most mothers feel when leaving their children, regardless of the child's age.

It's a special honor and privilege for me to be a part of any family's journey with the dying process of a loved one, especially when that family is one I already know and love. Being given the opportunity to bring a bit of comfort to my friend during an emotionally painful time is a memory I will always cherish.

From Jo Marie:

Words cannot adequately express the love and gratitude I feel for the comfort, support, and insight that Julie gave to me when my beloved mother went to be with our Lord. I feel God planted Julie in my life to ease my loss, emptiness, and fear during that time. Through her special gift, Julie allowed me to visualize what was transpiring as my mother passed from this world to the next, and for that I will be forever grateful. To this day, I will from time to time pull out the folder Julie prepared for me on my mother's passing and read through it. This continues to give me peace. Even though I still miss my mother, I know through my faith and Julie's words that my mother is happy and that she is still watching out for my family and me. Thank you, Julie, for sharing your special gift with me, as well as with others. God be with you and bless you always.

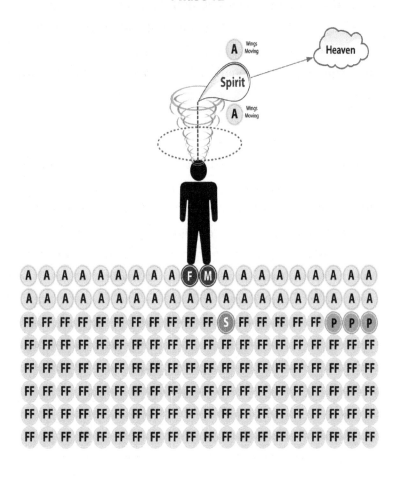

Miss Rose

Phase 12

F Father M Mother A Angel S Spouse FF Family & Friends P Pets

Chapter 9

The Whole Team for Jeanne

In July 2006, my dying father was in a coma at Riverside Hospital in Columbus, Ohio. The rest of my family did daytime duty, while I handled the several nights he remained in the Intensive Care Unit (ICU) before he passed. One night, when the nurses asked me to leave the room around 3 a.m. so they could bathe Dad, I went to the waiting area and started to read my book. Before long, a woman I had seen earlier in the evening sat down next to me. We introduced ourselves, and then I asked her how she was doing. She proceeded to tell me she lived in Northern California and was at the hospital with her family who had come in from all over the country. They were holding a vigil, waiting for her mother to die.

Denise Phoenix's mother, Jeanne Davis, had spent many days in the ICU before the doctors said it was time to take her off the respirator. Although the medical team had told the family Jeanne would die within 15 minutes of removing the tubes, 27 hours later, Jeanne was still alive. I explained my ability as a medical intuitive and told Denise that if I could help in any way, I'd be delighted to do so.

Denise asked if I'd be willing to come into her mom's room and I immediately agreed. The room was located in another ICU pod at the opposite end of the floor from my dad's room. Upon entering the room, I found Denise's siblings and their children camped out, surrounding Jeanne, who was comatose. Her breathing was labored. The family members were sitting in chairs, lying on the floor with blankets and pillows, and standing leaning against walls. It was so touching. I thought, *This is one lucky woman to have so many loved ones with her.*

Denise introduced me to her family and told them a little about why she had invited me. I scanned Jeanne and then scanned the room. Her mother's spirit was out of her body, with angels—their wings moving—on either side of it. Jeanne's parents' spirits were at her feet—her mother at her left foot and her father at her right foot. The angels were in a straight line at the foot of her bed with all the family and friend spirits behind them. A group of dogs' spirits was gathered to the right. She was in Phase 11 of the Twelve Phases of Transition.

I psychically asked Jeanne if she was ready to go, and she said no. I then asked her if she was in pain, and she again said no. I asked her if she saw all the angels and spirits of loved ones surrounding her. To this she said yes. I asked her if she knew her family was here with her, and she again answered yes. I then asked her if she needed anything to help her let go. She said she wanted everyone in the room with her when she left her body.

"Are there more family members not in the room?" I asked Denise.

"Yes," she told me. "They're spread out all over the hospital. Some are in the main lobby sleeping on couches, some are sleeping in the ICU family lounge, and some are in the cafeteria."

"Your mom wants all of you here in the room with her," I told Denise.

"Do we need to call the ones staying at her house and have them join us?" Denise's brother asked me. I psychically asked Jeanne the question, and she said no. I relayed the information and then excused myself, wished them all the best, and went back to my dad's room on the other end of the floor in the adjacent pod.

Within an hour, as I was sitting beside my dad's bed, holding his hand and reading my book, Denise came to the door and motioned for me to come out.

"We got everyone into mom's room just as you said to do and she died within ten minutes," Denise told me. "She was waiting for everyone to be with her. How can we ever thank you?"

I told her it was my privilege to meet her and her family and to help them. I then thanked her for allowing me to be a part of her family's experience.

Observations

Was it a coincidence that I happened to be in that hospital

on that day, at that exact hour, to meet Denise? Was it a co-incidence that Denise and her family were willing to allow a stranger who claimed to have psychic abilities into their dying mother's room? Was it a coincidence that her mother—who had been off of life support and in a non-communicative coma for 27 hours—died within ten minutes of having all of her family gathered around her, after I conveyed her wishes to them? Not a chance!

It's said we have a say in when we die and in who is with us when our spirits exit our bodies. From what I've seen and experienced, I agree.

Jeanne is a great example of how a dying person can con-trol their time of departure. She wanted the family members who were already at the hospital to be with her. She didn't want to wait until others arrived.

Does this mean she had her "favorites" with her when she finally died? Or could it mean she knew which family mem-bers could emotionally handle witnessing her death and chose to have them with her and spare the others? And was my in-volvement a parting gift from Jeanne intended to strengthen her family's faith in God and to reassure them that she would be fine after she died? Perhaps. After all, someone surrounded by and then carried off by angels would appear to be in good hands. Only Jeanne knows the answers to these questions.

From Denise:

By meeting Julie and having her check in with my mother to see where she was in her process of letting go, we all got to honor her final wishes for her departure into the nonphysical. It was an amazingly loving and wonderful experience for us! We all felt that Mother's soul had leaped out of her body, and we felt joy for her, knowing she was ready and we were there for support.

Julie helped us to know that many of the people in my mom's life who made their transition earlier were lovingly waiting for her on the other side. It was such a comforting thought, as was the visual description of the luminous angels in the room. Julie's help was a divine intervention! Instead of feeling deep sadness and grief, we were able to let go with peace and joy, knowing Mother was safe, loved, and happy in her new world.

Chapter 10

Farrell Finds Forgiveness

One Saturday afternoon in October a few years ago, I received a voicemail from Nena Robinson asking if I could scan her husband Farrell. Although Nena and I only knew each other socially, she had learned about my abilities from her daughter-in-law, my dear friend, Debra. Farrell had been admitted to the hospital with what his family thought was either a bad case of bronchitis or pneumonia.

I called Nena and then connected with Farrell. What I saw surprised me.

Farrell's spirit was out of his body, attached to the top of his head like the typical cartoon bubble I see in someone who is dying, and two angels were on either side of his spirit. His parents' spirits were at his feet and what had begun as a circle of angels had opened up into a horseshoe that ended at his shoulders—Phase 5 of transition.

Farrell psychically told me he wasn't ready to go and wasn't in pain. When I asked him what he needed, his response was, "I need to know my family loves me." When I asked him how he would know that, his answer was, "When they tell me."

Nena didn't seem surprised at what I saw. She is a very devout Catholic with deep spiritual beliefs. I sensed she had an idea her husband was dying, which was why she had asked to talk with me. Nena later told me she had told Farrell, "Julie says you're dying," and explained to him that his parents were present along with many angels. He seemed to accept and be at peace with the concept.

When I called her the next morning, she and other family members were at the hospital. At this point, the horseshoe of guardian angels had continued to open and was now at Farrell's waist. The angels positioned on either side of his spirit bubble had begun to move their wings, creating a vortex. Many more spirits were now in the room, as were the spirits of several dogs. He was now in Phase 9. I was surprised how quickly he had advanced from Phase 5 the night before.

Farrell psychically told me he still wasn't ready to go, he wasn't in pain, and he still needed to have his family tell him they loved him. Based on what I was seeing, I suggested to Nena that she consider having Farrell anointed (a Catholic ritual to bless the sick and dying) as soon as possible. She mentioned the family priest would be there in a few days, but considering how important the Catholic sacraments were to Nena, and based on what I was psychically seeing, I suggested she consider getting him anointed that day. The family priest could always anoint him again later if she wished.

By about 6:15 p.m., the horseshoe of angels was at Farrell's hips, many more spirits were present, and the angels' wings were still in motion, causing the vortex to become larger and stronger. He was now in Phase 10.

Farrell continued to tell me he wasn't ready to go. He said he needed to hear that Nena forgave him. As I spoke with Nena and relayed what I was experiencing, she seemed to understand what he wanted. In addition, Nena told me that immediately after speaking with me, a priest came walking down the hall looking for Farrell's room. She said she told her family, "Here comes one of Julie's angels."

By 6:00 a.m. the next day, the angels and Farrell's parents had formed a straight line at the foot of his bed. The two angels on either side of his spirit still had their wings in motion, causing the vortex above his head to continue to enlarge. The upward pull of the vortex had become very strong. He was firmly in Phase 11.

Farrell again told me he wasn't in pain and he wanted to go home to die. He also said he still wasn't ready to go as he wanted to see his grandchildren and needed to know Nena forgave him. Once I relayed this information to Nena, she said the family was gathering all the grandchildren in Birmingham. Some were in other states and one grandson was out of the country, but they were all en route.

When we spoke at 9:30 that evening, Nena relayed that Farrell had been transferred via ambulance to their home earlier that day. As I scanned Farrell, I told Nena he was in a holding pattern at Phase 11. The vortex continued to enlarge and increase in strength. More spirits continued to arrive and looked like dots on the horizon going out from behind the line of angels at Farrell's feet on both sides of the bed and also from the foot of his bed. I told Nena to consider all those spirits as the "Welcome to Heaven" committee.

At this point, Farrell told me he was ready to go but was waiting for the family. He asked me to tell them to hurry. He said he wasn't in pain but would like another pillow under his knees. He asked if he could have one of the new pillows Nena had bought on a recent trip to Atlanta. (She told me she had in fact just purchased pillows in Atlanta.)

Nena mentioned that after we had spoken earlier that morning, she went into Farrell's room and told him that if he forgave her for everything, she would forgive him. His response was, "It's worth dying to know you forgive me." What a response!

Nena said many of the grandchildren had been to see him already and that the remaining few would arrive the following day. I called Nena at dawn. At this point, Farrell's room was filled with a blindingly brilliant light. Farrell was still at Phase 11, waiting to depart. His spirit was in the vortex and the angels' wings on either side of his spirit were still in motion, creating a strong upward pull. The angels and his parents were still in a straight line at his bed. The spirits there to welcome him to Heaven were continuing to increase in all directions, and the spirits of his loyal dogs were still present.

Farrell told me he'd be ready to go once he saw the rest of his family and had a chance to say goodbye. Nena expected the remaining grandchildren to arrive shortly. I told her I believed Farrell was very close to dying, and that there was a good chance he wouldn't last throughout the day.

As I briefly spoke with Nena at 9:45 that night, I told her Farrell's spirit was beginning to exit the vortex and that I believed his passing was imminent. I also told her that thousands upon thousands of spirits were there to welcome him. Farrell told me he was now ready to go and he wanted Nena to know she was the absolute love of his life. I told Nena I believed he'd go before midnight. In fact, Farrell died around 11 p.m.

The next morning, I scanned Farrell and found nothing. I did a replay of his death and watched his spirit spring from the vortex as the two angels on either side of him turned him around. The wings that created the vortex now lifted his spirit up and to the right and escorted him to Heaven.

Observations

Although I had just recently met Farrell and several of his family members, I didn't know any of the particular history that defined their family. As the days progressed, I came to see just how cohesive a unit this family was and how their matriarch, Nena, was the glue that held everyone together. I found it remarkable how such a large group (six children, spouses, many grandchildren, and several great grandchildren) could transcend the inevitable past family dramas and focus on supporting one another during a difficult time.

Regardless of what had transpired over the years, Farrell dearly loved his family and they all obviously loved him very much. The fact that he wasn't ready to die until he said good-bye to each of his children and grandchildren was an indication of the depth of that love.

His granddaughter Sharrie later told me that on the last day of Farrell's life, he inquired about her car. He wanted to know if it was running smoothly. As he was preparing to die, Farrell's concern was for the welfare of his entire family and to obtain forgiveness from his wife. His expression of love for Nena was deeply touching. The fact that he allowed himself to quickly depart once he'd seen everyone is a testament to what our spirits can accomplish.

From Nena:

I could not have gotten through everything that happened without Julie. She gave me such peace.

From Debra:

Thank you for assisting us in understanding the process of Farrell's death. You made all of us feel more comfortable in accepting the inevitable. He left, but he went comfortably into his spirit being. It is so comforting to know that my amazing father-in-law and the best grandfather to my children knew how much we loved him. And this was all due to your insights!

Chapter 11

Precious Jade

Jade Grizzle was a young adult when she died. As a baby, she seemed to be developing normally until she was about 18 months old—when she, like most babies in the U.S., received vaccinations for a variety of serious diseases. The Centers for Disease Control reports that one in a million babies have severe problems after receiving the diphtheria, tetanus, and acellular pertussis (DTaP) vaccine. These problems can include long-term seizures, coma, lowered consciousness, and permanent brain damage. Jade was one of the unlucky few who made up the minority.

After one of these vaccines was administered, Jade experienced convulsions that caused permanent injury to her brain. When at the age of 20 she drowned in her bathtub, she had the mentality of a first-grader.

Jade's mom, Joyce, is deeply devoted to all four of her children and her two grandchildren. Long after Jade's siblings were old enough to bathe themselves, Jade still needed adult supervision. Each night, Joyce would help and watch over Jade as she bathed. Jade's last night, however, was different because while Joyce was gone from the bathroom for just a few minutes to change her clothes, as she had done many times before, Jade had a seizure and drowned in the tub. When Joyce returned, she found her daughter under the water and unresponsive. Both the paramedics and Joyce's husband Steve tried to revive Jade, but she was already gone.

Joyce and I spoke by phone a few days after Jade's death. Her older daughter, Jasmine, joined us on the call. Both women wanted to see if I could communicate with Jade's spirit to find out what had happened. I was delighted to try and also offered the option of doing an instant replay of Jade's death. They accepted. What I saw was unlike anything I'd ever previously seen.

First of all, both of Jade's parents and all of her grandparents were alive, so in keeping with the maternal line of spirits facilitating a death experience, Jade's great grandparents' spirits were present. I knew they were her maternal great grandparents because they were Japanese, and Joyce's mom (Jade's maternal grandmother) is Japanese, so her mother's parents must also have been Japanese. In fact, they were the spirits anchoring the circle of guardian angels around Jade as she was dying.

Secondly, Jade not only had the usual ring of angels around her, she had four additional rings! Because the spirits of Jade's family, friends, and pets were outside the five rings of guardian angels surrounding Jade's body, they were further from Jade than I normally experience. Jade's spirit was out of her body and attached to the top of her head and she had two angels on either side of her spirit. The movement of their wings caused the obligatory vortex and upward pulling vacuum to form.

While scanning the death scene, Jade told me she had had a seizure, lost consciousness, slipped under the water, and then her spirit watched the activities from above. Jade said her death was quick and painless. She said her spirit instantly evacuated her body and was supported by the two angels on either side. She told me she and the angels lingered quite a while after she died. She described how her stepfather Steve had rushed into the bathroom and had done his best to revive her. She talked about the paramedics arriving, how they, too, tried to revive her, and how they took a long time to carry her body out of the house. Her descriptions were those of someone who had actually witnessed their own death scene. Amazed, Joyce and Jasmine confirmed these details.

Jade said she owned a locket she wanted her sister Jasmine to have. "Tell Jasmine to go get my necklace," Jade relayed. I mentioned this to Joyce and Jasmine, and Jasmine asked if it was the one with the purple stones. Jade replied, "No, the locket." Joyce and Jasmine didn't know what Jade was talking about. They didn't remember a locket, so they went and looked in Jade's jewelry drawer. There, they found an old locket someone had given Jade when she was little. Inside the locket, they found a picture of Joyce and one of Jasmine. Of all her possessions, the locket with pictures of the two most important people in her life was what Jade wanted her sister to have.

Jade also told me that she was an emissary sent to educate those around her. Jade said she was sent to teach peace, unconditional love, tenacity, and sanctity. I understood the peace, unconditional love, and tenacity parts. Those caring for Jade had needed and in fact exhibited those attributes. The sanctity part of the equation was a bit baffling to me. I'd always thought of sanctity in a religious or theological way. When I looked the word up to get its exact meaning, the dictionary definition said, "The quality or state of being holy, very important, or valuable." Joyce, Jasmine, and I all agreed that Jade showed everyone in her life how important special needs people can be.

Observations

Joyce is the friend I mentioned in the introduction who gave me *Anatomy of the Spirit*—the book that started me on my spiritual journey. The inscription she wrote says, "In May of 1997, to my dear friend Julie, here's some soul food. May your own personal power continue to grow, healing and nurturing yourself and others. Thanks for your wisdom, ear, and sometimes shoulder for me to cry on. I feel so blessed to have you as a friend. Love and light, Joyce."

Joyce gave me this book almost ten years before her daughter died. At that time, I had no clue I was psychic let alone that I had the ability to identify medical conditions, facilitate energetic healings, communicate with spirits both alive and dead, and see angels, spirits, and energy fields. I didn't even know such abilities existed.

Is it a coincidence the woman who provided the impetus for me to explore energy medicine would benefit from my skills ten years later at the death of her own daughter? Not a chance! Through this experience, Joyce has taught me to communicate the information I receive regardless of how wacky it may seem. After all, in the end, I'm only the messenger. It's the prerogative of the person receiving the information to do what they wish with the information.

Jade was an extraordinary person. She could occasionally be a challenge to her family and caregivers, and at the same time she was remarkably loving to everyone she met. Keeping Jade in a nurturing, caring home surrounded by protective and encouraging family members allowed Jade to thrive.

The never-before-seen presence of so many circles of angels at her death leads me to believe she was most likely a heavenly emissary. She was indeed a representative sent on a mission. People who knew her all seem to agree she had a special effect on everyone who met her. Is it possible we as a society need to pay closer attention to special needs people? What can they teach us, and what special lessons are they trying to impart? Do we give them the same respect we give unchallenged folks?

I believe we're all put in each other's paths for a reason. We're all part of the experience of each other's souls. We all play a role that teaches something. It's up to us to figure out what that something is and how to use the information we learn. I do believe Jade was a special messenger from God— both her life and her death confirm it.

From Joyce:
Julie completely changed my perception of Jade's passing. Rather than looking upon the actual event as horrific, which was how I initially perceived it, she helped me see it as a holy and even beautiful experience by describing what she saw when Jade's spirit left this world. I will be eternally grateful to her.

Jade

Phase 12

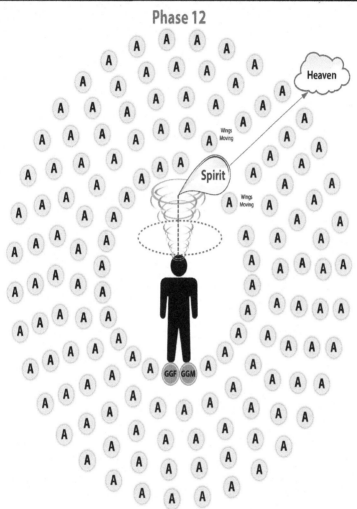

"Emissary" Sent To Teach:
Peace Unconditional Love Tenacity Sanctity

GGF Great Grandfather   GGM Great Grandmother   A Angel

Chapter 12

Marlene Makes A U-Turn

*M*arlene Fournet was the mother of my friend, Trish Fournet Dugger. Marlene was an original. She was strong-willed, opinionated, fun, and she loved her family. At the age of 69, Marlene suffered a stroke while having surgery and was put on life support. Trish flew from her home in Louisville to Kansas City to be with her mom.

Trish, a veteran emergency room nurse, didn't have high hopes her mother would survive long. As Trish had expected, when she arrived at the hospital, she found her mom in the Intensive Care Unit, connected to a ventilator and unresponsive. Over the next few days, the doctors and medical staff let the family know they didn't expect Marlene to recover and recommended she be removed from life support. After much heart-wrenching discussion, the family agreed and Marlene was taken off the ventilator.

All along, I was scanning Marlene and reporting my findings to Trish. From what I was seeing, Marlene looked as though she was in the final phases of transition. As usual, each time I checked on her, I'd ask her if she was ready to go, but each time, she'd say no. When I asked her what she needed, each time her reply was the same: "I need to see Trish."

By this time, Trish had flown back to Louisville. When I told her that her mother needed to see her before she would allow herself to die, Trish said, "I can't be there. I'll go back for the funeral."

The story remained the same over the next several days. Each time I scanned Marlene, she was in Phase 11. Her spirit was out of her body, she was surrounded by guardian angels, the vacuum above her head was large and had a strong upward pull, and the two angels on either side of her spirit were in position with their wings in motion, ready to escort her spirit to Heaven. She was off life support and was still hanging on of her own volition.

Then early one morning, I scanned Marlene while still lying in my bed. She was the same, but what I was about to see amazed me. I witnessed my spirit exit my body at the top of my head and fly to Louisville, where I watched Trish's spirit exit her body and join me. We then both instantly flew to Shawnee Mission Hospital in Overland Park Kansas, arriving at the hospital, just outside of Marlene's room. I stayed in the hall while Trish went in to speak with her still-comatose mother. When Trish was done, she joined me in the hall, and we both flew back to Louisville. I dropped her off at home, watched Trish's spirit get back into her body, and then I flew home and watched my spirit get back into my own body. I had never experienced anything like that before!

Once again, I scanned Marlene—and this time, I saw her

spirit lift out of her body and the angels on either side of her carry her up and to the right. I assumed she was headed for Heaven. I looked at the clock, saw that it was 5 a.m., and made a mental note to call Trish to let her know.

Time in the spirit world isn't necessarily the same as time in our human world. In most instances, when I see a person in one of the phases of transition, even when I see their spirit exit their body, it's happening in what we know as our linear, human, time frame. Sometimes, however, I see things happen in the spiritual reality before they happen on Earth, so I didn't know if Marlene was about to die or if she was already dead.

I talked with Trish later that morning, relaying what I had seen, and told her I fully expected she'd soon receive a call telling her about her mom's passing. I told her I loved her and was available to her at any time.

At about 2:30 p.m., as I was waiting to pick Jonathan up from school, my cell phone rang. It was Trish. "Jules," she said. "The angels brought her back!" As I had predicted, Trish received a call from the hospital—but the news was that Marlene had awoken from her coma!

For the next five minutes or so, I psychically communicated with Marlene in Kansas City while I talked via cell phone with Trish in Louisville—all while I was in the St. Rose Academy carpool lane in Birmingham. It was like a sci-fi conference call!

Trish had me psychically ask questions like, "Mom, did you die and come back?" The answer was yes. "Do you remember the angels carrying you off?" Again, the answer was yes. When Trish asked her mother why she had come back, Marlene answered, "Because I want more time with Bill [her husband]."

I asked Marlene if she was in pain, and she replied, "a little." Then Trish wanted me to ask her if she was hungry, to which her mother responded in typical Marlene fashion, "Hell yes, I'm *starving!*"

Within a couple of days, Marlene was well enough to be transferred to a nursing home, where she lived for another two years. Although she was paralyzed on her left side, she very much wanted to live. She told Trish as much several times throughout the next couple of years. She kept mentioning she wanted to spend more time with Bill.

When once again Marlene seemed to be dying, Trish was in Hawaii on vacation. She called me from Hawaii and told me she was considering whether or not to go to Kansas City. I scanned her mom and saw that she was in Phase 10. Marlene psychically told me she was ready to go, wasn't in pain, and needed Trish. This time, Trish left her family on vacation, flew to Kansas City to be with her mom, and was joined by her college-aged daughter, my goddaughter Lauren, who had driven in from Louisville. From the time Trish got to the nursing home, Marlene lasted about 36 hours. At the time of Marlene's passing late at night, Trish was the only one with her.

Observations

Did Marlene actually die the first time? I don't know for

sure. I do know I watched her spirit exit her body when it disconnected from the top of her head, and I watched the angels escort her up and to the right.

Did Marlene get to Heaven and find out it wasn't her time? Perhaps. Was it her decision to come back or was she told to return and live? Only she and God know the answers to those questions.

When she finally died, Marlene got her wish that Trish be with her. The first time, she repeatedly told me she was waiting for Trish. We thought she needed Trish to physically go to her, however, once Trish's spirit visited her, Marlene awoke from her coma within a few hours. Can our spirits actually nurture those we love telepathically? It looks like Trish did.

And what about this astral travel I experienced with Trish? Can our spirits actually travel to different times and places? My answer to that question is a resounding *yes!* I have done it many times and have been able to describe places, eras, people, clothing, and more—only to have my observations validated later either by individuals or historical records. Some people believe we all experience astral travel (also known as astral projection) when we sleep.

Have you ever felt as if you were falling while dreaming? It's said that's when our spirits come back into our bodies after astral travel.

What I do know for sure after this experience is that we never know when it's someone else's time. Even when we think the end is imminent, when we're absolutely certain our loved one will die any minute, it doesn't always happen the way we expect.

Life, as well as death, is still filled with surprises.

From Trish:

Having Julie communicate with Mom on her journey into her next life eased a heavy heart. It reinforced my belief that there is a force out there larger than us all. I am so blessed to have Julie in my life.

Chapter 13

Soulmates in Life and Death

$\mathcal{M}$ost of us have either heard about or know of a couple who, after many years together, died at about the same time. John and Mary Hawkins were such a couple. John grew up in Seattle, and Mary was reared on a farm in Pennsylvania. They were both music majors when they met in college. In June of 1942, shortly after their graduation, they married.

Mary was devoted to her family and enjoyed cooking and entertaining. John was completely devoted to Mary and enjoyed playing tennis and the piano every day. The two were inseparable for close to 70 years.

Late in their lives, as John entered the early stages of Alzheimer's, their family realized they needed to move to an assisted living facility. So their ever-devoted daughter-in-law, my friend Suzy Hawkins, made the arrangements. Suzy oversaw the sale of the Hawkins' home, the downsizing of their possessions, and their move three hours north to be closer to the rest of the family. All this was a huge change for Mary and John, but one that everybody, including Mary and John themselves, knew was needed.

After a few months, the family realized that John was going to require additional supervision in order to keep him safe. They opted to have John live in the secured Alzheimer's side of the assisted living facility while Mary remained in the couple's apartment at the same complex. This was the first time since they were married that they had lived apart. Both John and Mary were miserable.

Sensing this, Suzy found another option for them: a board and care facility where they could be together and receive both the care they needed as well as the security that John now required. These living arrangements lasted for about a year and seemed to satisfy their desire to be together.

In the second week of January, 2010, Suzy called to let me know Mary wasn't doing well. I told her I'd keep an eye on Mary from Alabama and that I'd keep her posted. When I first scanned Mary, she was in the early phases of transition with a marked nuance—a double row of angels was encircling her. I didn't know exactly why that was so, but I figured more interesting developments would most likely come in the days ahead.

When I scanned Mary on January 15, the day she died, I saw that she was in Phase 11. Her spirit was out of her body in the spirit bubble configuration with angels on either side of it. The vortex funnel had formed above her head and had a very strong upward pull. Her parents' spirits were in the usual places. Mary's dad was wearing a black suit, white shirt, and dark tie, and he was positioned at Mary's right foot. Mary's mother was at her left foot and was clothed in what looked like a work dress with a full apron over it. Angels stretched in a straight line on either side of Mary's parents.

The second circle of angels had formed a horseshoe shape with the open ends at Mary's shoulders. This horseshoe of angels intersected the line of angels at her feet. It's rare that I see angels standing in the human zone (on the other side of the angelic line of demarcation).

Hundreds of spirits were also in attendance. As is often the case, so many family and friends' spirits were present that they looked like specs on the horizon. In the animal section, I saw dogs, cats, cows, sheep, pigs, chickens, and even baby chicks (which wasn't surprising considering Mary grew up on a farm).

I was astonished to see that John's spirit was present and standing at Mary's right shoulder—even though John was still alive! Nevertheless, there he was, supporting his beloved wife as she was preparing to leave her body. He was on the human side of the angelic line.

As I watched the replay of Mary's death, what I witnessed was extraordinary. The vortex above her head was massive and extremely powerful. It had what felt like a thousand times more upward pull than I normally feel. Mary's vortex created gusts of wind that circled her bed, similar to the way a tornado whips up wind as it spins. I hadn't ever seen or felt this phenomenon before. Usually, the wind patterns of the Phase 12 vortex are only in an upward direction.

Next, the horseshoe of angels intersecting the line of angels at Mary's feet seemed to be acting as a wind shield to contain and control the gusts. Having the u-shaped line of angels in place helped focus the wind energy and caused it to increase in velocity like a centrifuge. I'm no physicist, but I've seen how an object spinning in a circle gains momentum and creates energy, much like how a turbine or jet engine does.

The centrifuge created by the vortex above Mary's head and the position of the angels created a spinning energetic force of immense power. It was moving so fast that it appeared as a blur. When I asked how long the centrifuge had been rotating at that speed, I was told it had been spinning at that rate for more than two hours.

When Mary's spirit finally exited her body, it blasted off like a small but really fast rocket. Once her spirit was separated from her body, Mary's two guardian angels, who had been on either side of her spirit, turned her around and escorted her upward and to the right toward Heaven.

After Mary died, even though John was still in the early stages of Alzheimer's, he seemed to understand his wife was gone. In most ways, his behavior stayed the same. His health was stable. He could dress and feed himself, and he continued to play the piano every day. Although John's family sensed how much he missed Mary, they were prepared to give him the care he needed for what they assumed might be a number of years.

Imagine their shock when they received a call exactly 13 days after Mary's death informing them John had suffered a seizure at dinner. Suzy and her husband, John, Jr., met the elder John at the hospital. Suzy called to let me know. I told her that she and the family were in my prayers, that I'd scan John from Alabama, and that I'd keep her posted. John died the next day, less than 24 hours after his seizure.

When John was in Phase 11 and close to departing, his dad (who was dressed in a black suit, white shirt, and dark tie) was at his right foot. John's mother wore a very stylish mint green chiffon dress and was positioned at his left foot. Angels stretched out into a straight line from both sides of his parents. Behind them was a line of 14 women. Mary was in the spouse spot, behind and to the right of John's mother, and the rest of the women were relatives. A line of only women behind the angelic barrier? I hadn't ever seen that before. What was up with that? Was John a true babe magnet? Since I knew John was an only child, I inquired as to who the rest of these female spirits were and was told that they were his aunts and great aunts. I was told he was the type of male whom women loved to nurture.

On the other side of the angelic line, John's spirit was out of his body attached to the top of his head and had three angels surrounding it. I found that interesting, since I normally see only two guardian angels. The vortex was in place above his head and the upward pull was being generated from the movement of all three angels' wings.

Most people's spirits look like a hologram of them. If you've seen the Star Trek television show or movies, think about how people look when they're being "beamed up" to another planet or galaxy—their form gets almost transparent, like a hologram. That's what a spirit normally looks like to me. And it feels like air.

Well, not John's spirit! It reminded me of Gumby! As John's spirit was in the process of exiting his body, it had a rubbery consistency that was bendable and stretchable. It took a long time to exit the vortex because as the upward pull would help the upper part of his spirit emerge—say, from his shoulders up—the lower parts of his spirit would remain in the funnel. As soon as part of his spirit was out of the vortex, it'd be pulled back in. It was a struggle. His spirit would twist and turn, trying to evacuate the spinning energy, but his efforts seemed fruitless. As I watched, I understood why John had three guardian angels assisting his spirit in disconnecting from his body—extra muscle was needed.

At the same time, John's spirit seemed confused. It was as if something vital was missing, and although John didn't know what that was exactly, he was looking for it. Then, all of a sudden, I watched as Mary's spirit left the line of female relatives behind the angelic line of demarcation and repositioned itself next to John's right shoulder. (I noted with interest that the position was the same location John occupied as he assisted Mary at the time of her death.) Once John realized she was there, his spirit relaxed and was able to easily flow through the vortex and separate from his body. His spirit then joined the three angels hovering above who turned him around as they, along with Mary's spirit, flew up and to the right toward Heaven.

Observations

Do soulmates really exist or are they some sort of Hollywood creation? I know soulmates do in fact exist because I've accessed countless past-life experiences for clients and for myself, where dates, times, and other facts have been verified. Soulmates appear in different roles in each lifetime. Our soulmate in one lifetime could've been our parent, sibling, friend, spouse, child, business associate, lover, and so on in another lifetime. Have you ever met someone and immediately felt as if you've known them your whole life? It's highly probable you and that person were together in a past life or lives.

I believe John and Mary were together in many, many, past lifetimes and that they came together as romantic soulmates and spouses this time around. When they were alive, everyone who knew them would tell you they were indeed inseparable. Some people may have thought John was henpecked or overly controlled by Mary. He couldn't have cared less what anyone thought. John was totally and completely enthralled with and devoted to his wife. I believe their bond in this lifetime was forged over all the lifetimes they had already spent together, so of course it didn't make sense to a lot of people. Those folks just didn't understand because they didn't have enough information and because they hadn't ever experienced a similar situation in their own lives.

John and Mary were also terrific role models. John, Jr., and Suzy have been happily married for 45 years and are devoted to each other, their children, and their grandchildren.

For the 30 years that I've known them, John and Suzy have displayed an extraordinary bond much like that of the senior Hawkins'. Psychologists tell us our parents influence our behavior, even into adulthood. I tend to believe the shrinks.

To the end, John was the ultimate gentleman. He let his wife go first, even in death, and then fourteen days later, he joined her. Some may say John died of a broken heart. I tend to believe his life's work was done and he chose to join his soulmate for whatever would become their next adventure together. And what about Mary? In death as in life, she supported her husband until the very moment his spirit left his body. By showing John she was there for him, she helped comfort him and ease his transition from this life into the next. And then they went to Heaven together.

I guess I shouldn't have been surprised by what I witnessed as I replayed John's death, but I was. Maybe I should've expected John's dying experience to have had interesting nuances, since Mary's had as well. What I have learned from this couple and from the 20-plus years I've been doing this work is to not have expectations. Every person's passing has its own glorious components.

From Suzy:
   Julie's observations and support during the simultaneous passing of my in-laws was both fascinating and comforting. Her friendship over the years has been a blessing.

Chapter 14

The Train Wreck

One weekday evening I met my friend Steve at his office building to deliver some documents. His colleagues had all gone home by the time I arrived, and he was working alone in his office.

From the street, the one-story building looked fairly small and non-descriptive. But inside, the space appeared much larger since in addition to the main level, it had a basement with office and conference room space. Steve had told me he and his coworkers believed the building was haunted. He would often regale me with tales of hearing footsteps in the hallway, doors opening and closing by themselves, and papers rustling late at night when he was working alone in the building. I always listened with interest and acknowledged his experiences, although the few times I had been at his office during normal business hours, I hadn't ever encountered any paranormal activity.

None of that was on my mind when I arrived that evening, although ironically, a storm had begun to brew. After a few minutes of casual conversation, Steve suggested I accompany him as he made his rounds through the building to turn off the lights and make sure all of the doors were locked. As we walked down a flight of stairs into the lower level, we continued to casually chat about our day. Then, when we reached the lobby, Steve asked if I felt anything.

"Like what?" I responded.

"You know," he said. "Do you sense any spirits or ghosts hanging around? You remember those stories I've told you about—I was just wondering if you could pick anything up." I hadn't seen or felt anything, but I also didn't have my radar on for picking up that sort of thing.

"Let me tune in," I suggested.

As we walked to the first set of offices, I scanned the room and saw the spirit of an Indian Chief standing in the corner. The chief was wearing a full headdress of colorful feathers that went from the tip of his forehead, across the top of his head and stretched down to the ground. He was clothed in a tan-colored suede shirt and long pants and was wearing tan moccasins. He was from the Lakota tribe in the Dakota territories (which is now the states of North and South Dakota).

Although I was a bit startled to see the spirit of an Indian chief, I wasn't ever afraid. He was regal and very matter of fact—not at all threatening. The chief and I communicated telepathically. He told me his name was Rolling Thunder and he was there to provide guidance for those exploring new territories. I figured that meant new product areas of business. Interestingly enough, Steve was the company's chief strategy officer, the one who guided the company into new phases and niches of the business. (Another interesting synchronicity was that long before we met, both Steve and I had briefly lived in the Dakotas--he in North Dakota and me in South Dakota.)

Steve had apparently used this office when he first joined the company, and assuming the chief just hung out in this office, I wondered if the chief was one of his spirit guides. Now, I absolutely believe that to be true because I've subsequently seen the chief with Steve in other locations, including some that were out-of-state.

I felt like a translator between the chief and Steve. I would ask the chief a question, either silently in my head or aloud so both Steve and I could hear it, and the chief would answer me telepathically. I then relayed verbally to Steve what I heard the chief say in my mind. Likewise, when Steve asked a question aloud, I would hear the chief's answer in my head and then tell Steve what he answered. After spending a few minutes with Chief Rolling Thunder, we proceeded on our locking-up tour through the building.

As we walked down one hallway, there was a bank of windows and a door leading to the outside on our left and a doorway into the mailroom on our right. By this time, the storm was getting pretty intense, with loud thunder accompanied by lots of lightening that illuminated our surroundings each time it streaked against the sky. It was beginning to feel like a ghost busters adventure!

We stopped inside the hallway and faced the mailroom door. It was now dusk so the room was dimly lit except for the frequent flashes of lightning. Since my radar was still on, I immediately saw what looked like a makeshift morgue. Bodies covered in white sheets were lying extended from the walls on either side of the hallway—more than 30 corpses in all, neatly arranged. Ghosts in turn-of-the-19th-century dress walked down the aisles, attempting to identify their loved ones. Some of the ghosts wore denim overalls and carried shovels, axes, picks, and other tools, while other ghosts searching the morgue were nicely dressed in what was probably their Sunday best.

In asking several of the ghosts what was happening, I learned there had been a train accident close by. The train had derailed and killed or badly injured several of the passengers. The men dressed in overalls were local townspeople there to assist, while those dressed in fancy clothes were passengers looking for missing loved ones.

At one point, the door to our right, leading from the basement lobby into the hallway, opened on its own and the ghost of a lovely young woman walked into the area. She was dressed in a floor-length green velvet skirt and matching waist-length jacket with a high-collared, starched white blouse, and she wore long white gloves.

This *did* freak me out a bit—Steve had experienced doors opening on their own before, but this was my first time. The energy around and inside my body was vibrating so fast I could actually hear a buzz in the room. The hair on the back of my neck and arms was standing straight up and I had a huge case of chill bumps. And of course, the storm was still violently raging outside. I felt as if I'd stepped into some sort of real-life scary movie.

The woman told me her name was Betsy. She was tall and slim and looked to be in her early thirties. Her brown hair was styled in a Gibson Girl updo and she had a small but stylish green velvet hat perched on top of her head. Normally, I'd expect someone with this description to act like an aristocrat, but this woman was totally panicked.

In my mind, I telepathically overheard her ask a man in overalls carrying a shovel if he'd seen a little girl in a pink dress. She told him that she and her four-year-old daughter Sally had been passengers on the train and were separated when it derailed.

There was a lot of commotion happening. Townsfolk and passengers were milling about trying to make sense of what had happened, while locals carried the bodies of the deceased into the room on stretchers and placed them with the other corpses.

I continued to relay all I was seeing, hearing, and experiencing to Steve. I felt like a news reporter describing the scene of a tragedy as it was unfolding. I'd read about multiple realities happening simultaneously and found myself and my friend smack in the middle of at least two. At that point, Steve asked if I could help the ghosts go into the light (go on to Heaven), and I told him I'd try.

The next thing I knew, the wall in front of us, the one without windows, seemed to disappear (almost as if a large industrial overhead garage door had opened) and a wall of brilliant white light tinged with a bit of yellow appeared. I had seen this wall of light many times and knew it was the entrance to Heaven.

Once this passageway to Heaven appeared, I began to watch the ghosts walk toward it and enter. They moved as though a magnetic force was guiding them into the light. The corpses covered in white sheets that lay on the floor seemed to vanish. They didn't rise up and join the others in a procession to the light. I believe their spirits were already in Heaven. They had fulfilled their life's lessons and purpose and had chosen to remain in the light while the others had chosen to remain in ghost form to continue learning.

Meanwhile, I noticed some paranormal commotion coming from a conference room to our left and mentioned it to Steve. Just then a group of beings resembling the dementors from the Harry Potter movies flew in and formed a circle above our heads that encompassed most of the hallway where we were standing. *Yikes!* I thought. *What the heck are those?* Once again, every hair on my body stood up and I was awash in chill bumps. I related what was happening to Steve and asked him to stand next to me so the two of us could form a protective shield. Although these new arrivals certainly looked spooky (dark figures without faces wearing long, hooded capes that flowed behind them as they swooped around), I knew intellectually that they couldn't harm us. I sensed that their energy vibration was very low and that they represented negative emotions and behavior.

"What happens in that room?" I asked Steve.

"We call it the War Room," he answered. "It's where we

have company meetings about strategy, personnel, problem solving, whatever—pretty much anything having to do with the running of the company."

"Are people ever nasty to one another in there?" I asked.

"Yes, there can be a fair amount of backbiting, posturing, dishonesty, and manipulation between executives and managers," he explained. "It can get very negative in there."

At that point, I understood that the dementor-like figures were symbolic of the energy of all of those negative emotions stored in the physical walls and furniture of this conference room. And I knew if I raised Steve's and my personal vibrational levels very high, I could dissipate them.

And that's exactly what I did. I shot the highest vibrating energy I could through myself and into Steve and watched beams of white energy emit from us and zap each cloaked figure, which caused them to immediately evaporate. It was as if by raising our vibrational levels, Star Wars light saber-like beams of energy eradicated the surrounding negativity. It's like how walking into a dark room can feel a bit creepy but once you flick on the light, the room suddenly feels much better.

"This is some wild stuff you've gotten me in to!" I told Steve, relieved that the creepy figures were gone. In fact, by this point, all of the ghosts from the makeshift morgue had entered the light, and with the dementor-like beings eradicated, the scene had gone back to a normal, present-day office building. Amazed at what had transpired over the previous half hour, Steve and I decided to go back upstairs.

As we began walking through a small hallway leading to the stairs, I started getting an odd feeling—although I didn't initially see anything unusual.

"There are more ghosts here," I told Steve. "I can feel them." When I scanned the area, I discovered they were hiding in the space above the drop ceiling tiles. They looked like former slaves. All were of African-American descent and all were dressed either in casual or work clothes. They included men, women, and children of all ages—and I quickly realized I was seeing several families. Steve and I stopped directly under the area with the spirits and I telepathically asked them to come down from the ceiling.

"No!" I heard several of them answer. One man's voice very clearly said, "We'll get shot!"

"By whom?" I asked.

"The train's conductor," came his answer.

Over the next couple of minutes, I had a telepathic conversation with the ghost of a man named Reginald who seemed to be talking on behalf of the group. I learned the families were in fact former slaves and were stowaways on the train. They were headed north in the hope of finding work and better living conditions. I finally convinced Reginald and his friends to come down from their hiding place. I told him he and the rest of his friends were ghosts and that I could help them get to Heaven and be reunited with their loved ones. I showed him the wall of light the other ghosts from the train accident had entered.

I was comfortable with this group of ghosts. Their energy

as a group felt soothing in a familiar way. Even though they were technically breaking the law, it felt as if I had met a group of friendly, trustworthy, and honorable people.

Next thing I knew, a hinged panel opened downwards from the ceiling revealing stairs leading to the floor. It was similar to the drop-down staircases found in homes that make attics accessible.

One by one, what ended up being twenty-seven ghosts walked down the energetic stairs. Steve and I were standing to the left of the bottom of the steps which caused each ghost to walk around us and then proceed through the wall of light to Heaven.

Men, women, and children ranging in age from infants to teen agers descended down the ceiling staircase. As they passed us, many of them said, "Hi Mr. Steve, or Hey Mr. Steve". The others just nodded their heads as they went by. It was obvious they all recognized and knew Steve by name.

The last one to come down was Reginald. He was a big, muscular man who resembled a 45-year-old version of the actor James Earl Jones. Reginald had dark hair sprinkled with specs of gray, wore a white shirt, tan pants held up with black suspenders, carried a dark jacket, and had a big smile on his face. Being in his presence felt comfortable in a warm and fuzzy familiar kind of way.

He thanked us for our assistance and stopped to talk for a few moments. Reginald said the train hit something on the track causing it to derail. He and his fellow stowaways had paid the train's conductor to smuggle them to the North. They had been allowed to hide in the baggage cars. They all just wanted a better life for their families and themselves. Some had relatives in Detroit who were going to help them find work.

Reginald told me he and his friends, while hiding above the ceiling tiles, had been watching the people who worked at the company and proceeded to tell me who Steve could trust. He mentioned several employees by name and would say things like, "Stay away from that one", and "She can be trusted". I would relay Reginald's commentary to Steve which prompted him to begin asking about certain colleagues. Who knew a ghost could act as a secret agent and provide inside intelligence?

As Reginald stood at the bottom of the staircase next to Steve and I, he continued to go through a litany of Steve's colleagues. Some of whom had offices in that building, some who had offices in other buildings owned by the firm. He mentioned each person by name and then mentioned things about that person that further identified he had been watching them. In his comments, Reginald gave Steve amazing insights as to what made a certain person act the way they did, and provided information as to how to best understand the person's mentality. The information he was giving Steve was invaluable both from a corporate and an interpersonal relationship standpoint. This information could be used to propel corporate projects and to find a way to please any resistors found in the group. These resistors could be thwarting the company's plans to move forward in different areas of expansion and could be roadblocks in the company's success. And since Steve was the chief strategy officer, it was up to him to devise a plan to accomplish the company's goals.

The most interesting part of this development was Steve instinctively knew in his gut which colleagues he could trust and which were to be avoided. Reginald's comments were validation for what Steve already knew. How can we utilize information from the spirits that surround us to better our lives? What's the easiest way to communicate with them? Is it in our best interest to follow their guidance? Is their guidance something our spirits already know? Is there a way to tap into our inner most selves in order to get guidance and advice?

All of these questions are valid and the answer to all of them is YES! First, how do we tap into our inner guidance? For some it's meditation or prayer. Getting still and blocking out the distractions we face every minute of every day. Silence your phone, your email notifications on your computers and tablets, and pick a quiet place where you can be still. Ask yourself a question and wait for the answer.

Another way is simply to ask yourself, "Is it in my best interest to ..." and finish the sentence with whatever. For example, "Is it in my best interest to talk with Sam about how we can get Tony to become more engaged in our conversations?" You'll get an answer in your head. It will happen as quickly as you can snap your fingers. If you think about it for more than a couple of seconds, it's your brain talking to you. Your brain's answer is acceptable and needs to be part of your overall gathering of information which will ultimately help you make a decision. In this instance however, I'm talking about a quick, easy, free, method of gathering outside advice. Seek the counsel of the spirits around you. After all, they have a bird's eye view of all that's happening, and all of the players. They also don't have any negative or ulterior motives towards you or anyone else for that matter. Since spirits are all goodness and light, they'll always have your best interest at heart.

This scenario was a real-time experience demonstrating multiple realities happening at the same time. We often treat a problem in our lives as a life and death situation and it rarely ever is. Spending the time witnessing the train wreck situation, reminded me of what sages have been saying since the beginning of time. Life is fleeting, so enjoy it. Don't sweat the small stuff because our soul (spirit) is eternal and we don't need to waste our time fretting over things out of our control. In the end, things always have a way of working out. Our spirits, along with God (the universe), have a much bigger plan for us in this human experience than we can ever imagine.

After all of the former slaves had gone into the light and the building was secured, Steve and I went to a local Greek restaurant. Outside, the rain continued to pour, and the thunder and lightning added to the drama of the night. We needed to spend some time dissecting what had just happened. What an experience. Even though at that time I'd been communicating with spirits for more than fifteen years, I'd never witnessed a scene like that before. And poor Steve, his head was spinning. I was grateful he had experienced what I had, otherwise, I'm not sure I could've or would've remembered everything that had transpired.

Multiple times throughout the evening I questioned my own sanity. Was I hallucinating, having a stroke or midlife crisis? As soon as I thought I was losing my mind, something would happen and be verified by Steve that instantly pulled me back into this other reality. As I often say, I can't make this stuff up. If I was that imaginative, I'd be the next JK Rowling (the author of the Harry Potter series) and be a billionaire.

Also, even though I knew the spirits couldn't harm us, I did feel safer having Steve with me. Perhaps having a partner in whatever endeavor, marriage, friendship, work, is in-bred in all of us. Are humans more like pack animals than we realize even in ghostly situations?

Over dinner, as Steve and I discussed the train wreck experience we had just shared, we felt as if we'd just watched a movie and somehow knew the characters personally. These were spirits in ghost form who were continuing to play out the lessons they still had to learn from this lifetime. They were all in their own purgatory. What we'd witnessed, gave me new validation for what I've heard many times before – our lives are just a big school, a school that gives us the opportunity to learn in a lot of different ways. There are no mistakes, just experiences on our learning curve. Since there aren't any permanent outcomes, we all have the ability to get it better next time. It's as if we live in an environment of eternal redemption. It's our mission to just create and learn from those creations. Is the outcome to our liking? Do we want to change it? What do we want it to be? If we knew we couldn't ever fail, what would we attempt? A new relationship? A new job? A new home? To change the relationship with loved ones already in our lives? If nothing was holding us back, what could we accomplish? The possibilities are endless.

By the way, just like the conference room in this story, buildings, furniture, and other objects can hold the energy of emotion. Tune into how a room, a house, or a building feels while you're standing in it. Does it feel calm or does it make you feel on edge? Likewise, pay attention to how an object feels when you hold it or how a piece of clothing feels when you touch it or try it on. We all have the ability to discern energy vibrations, we just have to begin to be aware that they exist.

Chapter 15

The Passing of Saint Pope John Paul II

$\mathcal{S}$ince multiple realities exist simultaneously, I can scan past, present, and future scenarios. That's exactly what I did with Pope John Paul II while watching his funeral on television.

Karol Wojtyla was born in 1920 in Wadowice, Poland, and died on April 2, 2005, in the Apostolic Palace in Vatican City. Made pope in 1978, John Paul II is known as one of the most traveled world leaders in history as well as the pope who helped end communist rule in Europe. He is widely seen as having significantly improved the Catholic Church's relations with other religions—particularly with the Jewish faith. Nine years after his death, Pope John Paul II was made a saint by the Roman Catholic Church.

As I watched John Paul's funeral, I replayed his death scene. To describe what I witnessed as extraordinary doesn't seem to give it justice. The scene was so astonishing that at the time I remember thinking, *This guy is either a saint or some kind of seriously enlightened prophet.*

As I began scanning the last moments of John Paul's life,

I noted a few familiar elements. His spirit was out of his body and appeared in the shape of a cartoon bubble attached to the top of his head. His mother was at his left foot and his father was at his right foot. That's where the normal angelic/spirit set-up ended.

The spirit of John Paul's older brother Edmund, who died of scarlet fever in 1932 at the age of 26, was between the spirits of his parents at the Pope's feet. I hadn't ever seen a sibling between parents before. The rest of the family and friends were positioned in a v-shaped section out from the Pope's feet. Usually, the family and friends section is a large rectangular shape and endlessly stretches out horizontally behind a line of angels at the foot of the bed.

In addition, hundreds of guardian angels were positioned on each side of the family and friends' section, stretching out in all directions. These angels surrounded John Paul and were visible as far as I could see. They all were kneeling on their left knees with their heads down, as if paying homage to the Pope.

John Paul's spirit seemed to emit a yellowish-white color that reminded me of the halos in old masters' paintings. In addition to the two angels on either side of John Paul's spirit, six more guardian angels hovered *above* his spirit in a horseshoe formation. A section of spirits of religious leaders extended out from his left shoulder and included rabbis, Greek Orthodox Patriarchs (popes), Eastern Orthodox popes, Muslim clerics, Archbishops of Canterbury, Episcopalian archbishops, Protestant leaders, Buddhist and Hindu monks,

African tribal leaders, and others I couldn't identify—all men. It fascinated me that these holy men occupied a special place, separate from the family and friends' section.

As the Pope neared death, the six angels in the arc above his spirit changed positions and encircled his spirit. Then their wings began to move in a slow, steady rhythm to create a vortex above John Paul's head. Since the wings of all six angels were in motion, the vortex formed quicker than normal. Soon, all of the hundreds of angels surrounding the Pope were on their feet and began to move their wings. As you can imagine, the drag of all those angels' wings created a tremendous vortex, and a large opening above John Paul's head appeared. The upward suction of the vortex was so strong that I could hear an audible whooshing sound that felt more powerful than the strongest tornado ever registered. The circular motion was dizzying to watch. The most interesting part of the whole scene was how reverent the slow, smooth, synchronized movement of hundreds of angels' wings felt. It was amazingly comforting.

Soon after the vortex appeared, a mass of cherubs (who appear to me as chubby little one-year-olds) floated over the whole scene, and 12 archangels, including St. Michael, encircled the vortex. Archangels appear to me as massive angels with enormous wings who are dressed in Roman warrior attire: short skirts, chest plate, sandals that lace up the calf, and a sword in a sheath hanging by their side. They're very muscular. (I would later learn that St. Michael is known as the Christian angel of death because it's believed he assists souls as they make their transition. John Paul apparently had a special devotion to him, and in 1994, he requested Catholics resume saying the Prayer to St. Michael at the end of Mass—a practice that had been suspended 30 years previously.)

Most people's spirits as they enter the vortex look like a hologram of their bodies, but not so with John Paul. His appeared as a mass of brilliant white-yellow light so powerful that as it exited the vortex, his spirit shattered it into tiny iridescent shards. Once his spirit finally emerged, it was surrounded by masses of archangels led by St. Michael and carried up and to the right to Heaven. I thought, *This is quite the spiritual Secret Service escort!*

After the replay of John Paul's death scene, I returned my attention to the television and scanned the funeral Mass as it was being broadcast. The funeral was attended by what was, at that time, the single largest gathering in history of heads of state outside of the United Nations. The group included four kings, five queens, at least 70 presidents and prime ministers, and more than 14 leaders of other religions. The total number of mourners was estimated to be more than four million (with a global audience of about two billion watching on television).

I expected to see the Pope's spirit with all of the clergy who were jointly officiating at the funeral Mass. What I found, however, was John Paul dressed in a priest's plain black cassock and Roman collar, standing in the crowd of regular folks in the middle of St. Peter's Square. An iridescent dry mist (which I believe is a representation of grace) floated in the air above and around all of the funeral attendees. I recognized this phenomenon from what I had witnessed when my own mother was dying.

Observations

Based on what I've read and heard, it would make sense the Pope was with the masses of people instead of the dignitaries at his funeral. He was a beloved, charismatic communicator (fluent in eight languages) who often conversed with the faithful in their native tongue. Do all saints, prophets, and spiritual leaders experience a death like John Paul's? I don't know for sure, but what I saw was so extraordinary, I can't imagine I will ever see anything like it again.

Saint Pope John Paul II

Phase 12

Heaven

Wings Moving

Spirit

Wings Moving

Father Mother Angel Religious Leaders FF Family & Friends Brother

Epilogue

I find it so fascinating to learn about someone's journey through life—the details relating to where they were born, their family of origin, their schooling, their choice of mates, their career, whether or not they decided to have children, and so on. All of these twists and turns in a person's life make them the perfect addition needed by the human race during whatever time they lived.

I believe that we all have a purpose and that we're all in this life to have the human experience and learn from it. Perhaps two of the most important lessons are to understand we're spirits in human form (all part of one collective body) and to learn how to treat one another with kindness and respect.

My life has been one amazing ride. I'm in awe of the life experiences I've been afforded in my fifty-plus years so far. Wife, mother, grandmother, daughter, granddaughter, sister, friend, businesswoman, inventor, medical intuitive—each role has had its own ups and downs, yet I wouldn't trade one minute of any of them.

As I embark on this new chapter in my life, publicizing what I "see" when someone is dying, it's my sincere hope that you and perhaps your family members will find comfort in

knowing angels and loved ones really do come to greet us—
all of us—and escort us to Heaven when we die.

Acknowledgements

This book happened with a lot of help from many people and I thank them all.

My editor extraordinaire, Katy Koontz, has become a dear friend. In addition to working on this book, we've been through the passing of loved ones, health opportunities, children graduating from college and going out on their own, and a multitude of other life events. Katy, I love you and am so grateful you're in my life.

All of the stories contained in this book are because of dear friends who have graciously agreed to let me into their lives during both calm and tumultuous times. I love you all and appreciate your allowing me to share your stories and for being such an important part of my life.

Several people proofread my manuscript and made suggestions that have been implemented on these pages. I am grateful to all of you for your efforts, love and support.

My teacher, mentor, and dear friend Susan Austin Crumpton, you will always have a special place in my heart and my life. For more than twenty years, you have guided me on a magical path I couldn't have ever imagined. Thank you for sharing your gifts with me and through me with the world.

Lastly, the centers of my universe, my husband Tim and

son Jonathan. Thank you for all of your encouragement, support, humor and love. You both are the lights of my life and I love you with all my heart.

About Julie Ryan

Julie Ryan is an inventor, entrepreneur, author, and medical intuitive. She works with individuals and healthcare providers to assist in diagnosing medical conditions and in facilitating healing. She also assists individuals and their families who have a loved one in the final stages of their lives as they progress through the dying process.

Over the past 35 years, Julie has founded nine successful corporations in various industries, including the medical, natural gas, long-term care, advertising, data security, and marketing fields.

Julie holds several patents and trademarks on surgical devices. Her inventions have been sold for more than 25 years throughout the world by her companies and through licensing agreements with global medical corporations.

For more information, or to schedule a private session or speaking engagement, or to listen to Julie's weekly podcast, please visit www.askjulieryan.com.

What People are Saying About Julie Ryan

I cannot express what a comfort and help it was to have Julie's guidance and intuitive sense in working with my brother, who was in a coma during his last days. The final few hours of his life were eased for us, as we had Julie sharing my big brother's wishes and desires. She shared with my sister and me details from my brother, our family, and my brother's life that she could have learned only from him! She truly is amazing and has a God-given gift.
—Kyle Rahn

I can never thank Julie enough for all her spiritual guidance in Mom's last week on this earth. It has made Mom's journey come alive for me with such a wonderful picture of where she is now!
—Melda Kautzmann

I give credit to Julie for helping me to tap into my inner self and feel that I had an awareness and peace like none other in my entire life.
—Christine Gonyea

Julie and I met for dinner and within one minute, she told me that my mother had started to move into the spiritual world. I was amazed at that, as I had not told her my mother had stopped eating. From then on, Julie would call me and comfort me by letting me know what phase my mother was in. She told me not to get scared or confused if my Mother started talking about and seeing her family members. Sure enough, Mother began telling me that her sister was with her and also that her parents were in the room with her. I would have been more upset and confused, but instead because of Julie's help, I was at peace with what was happening.
—Dudi DeBlasis

When Julie saw my father's mother and former pets around my father as he was dying, I felt very comforted.
—Cathy Bulich

First, I must say that I am a Christian and a believer, and I know that we must die to have eternal life. But as the end was near for my dad, I forgot everything that I believed, and I knew only that I was losing him to Alzheimer's. Julie was there for me throughout that journey. With her help, I knew that as he left us, he joined loved ones waiting for him. I can't thank Julie enough for the sense of peace that she gave me!
—Fran Stainback

With Julie's help, it was a great comfort to know that at the time of my father's death, he was greeted by all whom he touched and loved in this world.
—Angela Kirk, Ph.D.

Made in United States
North Haven, CT
31 August 2022

23504173R00104